To:

Emily

Peace Blessings

C J Thomas

Remembering Us: A Memoir

Published by: Cynthia Thomas, In Partnership with Nia Sadé Akinyemi, *The Literary Revolutionary.*

www.cjthomasauthor.com

www.theliteraryrevolutionary.com

Manufactured in the United States of America

Cover Design by: TLR Team

Edited By: Nia Sadé Akinyemi, *The Literary Revolutionary.*

www.theliteraryrevolutionary.com

ISBN #: 978-0-9968910-8-0

Follow Author Cynthia Thomas

Facebook.com/AuthorCynthiaThomas

Instagram/Twitter: @AuthorCynthiaThomas

www.cjthomasauthor.com

Remembering Us

By:

C.J. Thomas

PUBLISHED IN PARTNERSHIP WITH

The Literary Revolutionary

ATLANTA   MIAMI   NEW YORK   DMV   DALLAS   OKC

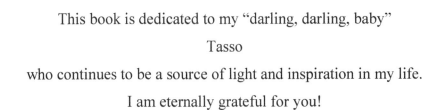

This book is dedicated to my "darling, darling, baby"

Tasso

who continues to be a source of light and inspiration in my life.

I am eternally grateful for you!

Author's Note: The details of Tasso's life experiences are being relayed to you from my memory as he told them to me during the 37 years we were together.

What therefore God has joined together, let not man put asunder.

Mark, Chapter 10, Verse 9

Acknowledgements

I would like to give thanks first and foremost to God, the Creator of all things. It is through my faith in God that I have been blessed with such an incredible story to tell.

To my oldest son, Ashuntu: You believed in me enough to order my laptop for me when you first heard me speak of how I needed one so I would not have to come downstairs to use the desktop . No more excuses!

To my oldest daughter, Ruby: Thank you for the design for my first website and for getting me up and running on the internet. You made it "get real" for me! Thanks for reminding me that I was already an author!

To the first half of the twin set, Jamaal: Thank you for your encouragement and for believing that not only could I tell this story, but that I would.

To my youngest daughter (and 2nd half of the twin set), Jamilah: Your suggestions and ideas helped give me direction, focus, and a point of view from which I could begin to write. Your perspective gave me the "kick-start" I needed to be able to tell this story. You have my eternal thanks!

To my youngest son, Ishaaq : There are not enough words to express my thanks for your countless, endless hours of technical support. Your patience surpassed anything I would have been able to tolerate! I could not have done any of this without you!

You all have my undying love and gratitude forever! -Mom

Contents

Dedication

Quote

Acknowledgments

Foreword

Section One - Tasso

Chapter One

Chapter Two

Chapter Three

Chapter Four

Chapter Five

Section Two - Cynthia

Chapter Six

Chapter Seven

Chapter Eight

Chapter Nine

Chapter Ten

Chapter Eleven

Chapter Twelve

Section Three- The Beginning

Chapter Thirteen

Chapter Fourteen

Section Four- "We" Began

Chapter Fifteen

Chapter Sixteen

Chapter Seventeen

Chapter Eighteen

Chapter Nineteen

Chapter Twenty

Chapter Twenty-One

Section Five- We Ended

Chapter Twenty-Two

Chapter Twenty-Three

Chapter Twenty-Four

Chapter Twenty-Five

Chapter Twenty-Six

Section Six-And Now....

Chapter Twenty-Seven

Chapter Twenty-Eight

Section Seven- Poems

Every Day

My Thoughts of You

Without You

I Miss You

It Hurts

Just When

Now

2017 Thomas Family Tree

Foreword

Tasso told me many times that I should write a book. I really did not pay him any mind, even though I should have. I realize now just how prophetic and intuitive he was. He never told me anything that wasn't true when it came to things in life, and everything he ever told me about people that I encountered in my life actually turned out to be true.

I had no idea that I had a writer in me. After Tasso died, words just started to come to me. I would often wake up in the middle of the night with ideas, thoughts, and words. I always thought I would remember them, but oftentimes I wouldn't. If I did, they somehow did not seem to have the same meaning. I learned to keep a pen and paper at my bedside to record my thoughts. Many times I would awaken throughout the night, write down my thoughts, get up the next morning and read them. I'd think to myself, *"Wow, that is a story or that is a poem."*

Telling this story is something I **have** to do. Even though it is a true story, it is coming **through** me from a higher power rather than **from** me. Those of you who believe in God will understand what I mean.

It is my hope that in reading our story, you will be entertained, enlightened, educated, and encouraged in some way to live out your life to its fullest; to follow your heart, to trust and believe in God, and to have no fear, even though there are times when you may be afraid.

May your life always be filled with joy, peace, and blessings for now and for always.

Part One

Tasso

Chapter One

Tasso was born July 25, 1949, in Loachapoka, Alabama, a small town located between Auburn and Tuskegee, Alabama. He was the fourth child born to Robert and Ruby Thomas. His parents were sharecroppers and he was one of those kids who did not go to school until October, as he had to stay behind to help with the work. Even though they did not have much in the way of material things, Tasso always spoke fondly of his mother and how much love he felt from her growing up. He attended school in a one room schoolhouse/church, which was common in rural communities at that time. When it was destroyed by fire, the students attended public school in Auburn.

Tasso told me that his father drank excessively and was somewhat abusive, yet he had fond memories of his childhood; of playing football, baseball, and basketball with his brothers. He spoke of how he was always trying to hang around and keep up with his older brother and his friends, only to be dismissed most of the time because they decided that he was too young to hang out with them (he was only one year younger). He would tell me how they would leave him behind and he would have to walk home from school and basketball practice along the railroad tracks by himself all the way from Auburn to Loachapoka. We often teased him when he told his "tales from the Dad side" as he went from walking one mile in the rain with holes in his shoes to walking ten miles barefoot in the snow!

Tasso was determined to have a better life for himself and did not want to get stuck in "Poka". He liked girls and they liked him, but he was determined not to become a father in high school like his brother and so many of his friends, so he stayed away from the ladies!

However, there was one girl in high school that he really liked. Tasso says she eventually dumped him for one of the more popular high school football players. Tasso took me to meet her when we were dating, as she had married the football player and they were living in Atlanta with their son. She and her husband (who eventually divorced) were among the first people who came to visit me at our home and brought condolences from their high school classmates when Tasso died.

When Tasso discovered his natural talent for playing basketball, he used that talent to get himself into college. He was accepted into Tougaloo College, in Tougaloo, Mississippi on a basketball scholarship. He had accomplished the first of many goals.... getting out of "Poka" and going to college!

Tasso and I first met in the spring of 1967 as he was preparing for his high school graduation and his entrance into college. I was entering high school. I will tell you more about this meeting later.

Chapter Two

Tasso attended college with a close friend from high school in Auburn who had also been granted a basketball scholarship. They were quite the "gangster pair" in college. He told me many stories of the freshmen and upperclassmen they terrorized on the small campus. He stated that so many of the upperclassmen from "up north" thought they were just "two dumb country hicks from Alabama" until they met them and found out otherwise. He was still not trying to venture into fatherhood at that time, so he kept his distance from the ladies. (I suspect if you talked to his friend, you might hear a different story).

He did tell me, however, that he was interested in this one girl in particular and one afternoon, she invited him to her house. Tasso told me that they were sitting in the living room, when he heard her father come into the house through the back door. He recognized the voice as that of his basketball coach! He panicked, and exited through the front door before the coach could see that he was trying to date his daughter! He knew he would be kicked off the team for good and his scholarship would go right out the window! From what I'm told, he never spoke to her again.

Tasso spent his summers working, trying to make money for the following school year. While he enjoyed making money, he recognized that working an ordinary job was not his vibe and he was always ready and anxious to return to school. He spent one summer in Boston, where he was staying when he wrote me a letter. He told me about the summer he spent in Atlanta with his brother and that they shared a small room somewhere in downtown Atlanta while he worked at a pie factory. He would never buy certain kinds of store bought pies as a result!

Tasso excelled in and enjoyed his studies at Tougaloo! It was there that he gained much knowledge about himself as a black man and about the history of black people throughout the world. He was very proud of the education he received at Tougaloo.

Tasso graduated from Tougaloo College on May 19, 1971, with a Bachelor's degree in History. He told me that he had no family support while he was in college. I can only imagine graduation day and how lonely it must have been for him with all the other graduates having family and friends to celebrate with them and him being all alone! Tasso was the first, and if I am not mistaken, the only one of his siblings to ever graduate from a four-year college. He had accomplished another goal....college graduation! He was extremely proud when he was able to obtain a copy of his degree to display on the wall in our home.

Chapter Three

After graduation, Tasso went to live with his sister and her family in New Jersey. His nephew was quite the street-wise young man, and was involved in the drug scene. Tasso's sister blamed him for her son's involvement in the street life and drugs, but his nephew was well into that life when he got there. Tasso stated that they would go out together only for his nephew to tell him he couldn't hang with him and would leave him on his own. Tasso did smoke weed and drink alcohol, but he never ventured into any other type of drug use as it was way too expensive and just not his thing!

Tasso taught high school in New Jersey, and worked at Seton Hall University as an instructor. For some reason, which he never disclosed to me, he decided to join the Army. He enlisted on June 13, 1973, and was assigned to Fort Dix, New Jersey, for his basic training. Joining the military was a decision he immediately regretted as he realized the rigors of military life did not suit him. He injured his back during basic training, was always absent from regular roll call, and was a regular in sick bay. He eventually made it through basic training and was assigned to a tour of duty in Germany.

In Germany, Tasso was assigned the duties of a clerk typist and then as a drug and alcohol abuse counselor. Tasso became close with his Colonel and other superior officers. They recognized the above average intelligence of this young man who was always challenging them regarding the basic rules of Army life. He told them that many of the rules did not seem to be logical or make much sense to him. He stated he challenged them on everything from diet to the reasoning behind why they were required to climb a mountain with a heavy field pack, only to reach the top, turn around, and come back down again. He was just not feeling it! Evidently, he always made a good argument for whatever he challenged them on as he was allowed to have a special, pork-free diet. Instead of regular field duty, he was assigned to his Commanding Officer as his personal driver!

It was during this time that Tasso was commissioned to write a poem for the reigning Miss Black America who was scheduled to visit their military base. He composed the poem, *"To a Brown Girl (Golden Lady)"*, which he read to her during the program when she was introduced to the troops on the base. He told me that, of course she was beautiful, she was impressed by his poem, and he had hopes of getting together with her after the program. However, either she or the commanding officers had other plans and the lowly private was not invited to the party! (Thank You, Miss Black America and Commanding Officers!) He spoke of this time as one of the highlights of his military career, even topping the awards and accolades he received for being a superior M-16 rifle marksman! Apparently, he was handy with a rifle as well as a pen!

It was during this time, that Tasso connected with one of his friends from Auburn. They had been both been assigned to the same military base during their tour of duty in Germany. They shared many an experience and adventure together during that time! They told me about a couple of their exciting "adventures". Judging from what I saw when the two of them got together, I am sure there are many others I would not even want to know about!

He remained a friend throughout our years together and we always considered him as family. The children came to know him as their "uncle" and we still keep in touch with him to this day. We allowed him to ride in the family limo with us on the day of Tasso's burial and he stood with Tasso's sons as they led us in the opening prayer at Tasso's memorial service.

Tasso around age 9   11th grade

TASSO THOMAS
Guard
Freshman, 5' 10", 151, Auburn, Alabama.
Tasso comes to the Bulldogs with a 26 game
point high school average. A fair ball player
in all categories, Tasso has the desire and
hustle to make it. He is also a member of the
great Bulldogs x-country team, and has great
potentials as a trackster.

TASSO THOMAS

Re-Printed from the Touglaoo College Sports Bulletin 1967-68

In Auburn, Alabama in the late 60's

To a Brown Girl
"Golden Lady"
I love you for your brownness
And the rounded darkness of your breast

I love you for the shadows
where your wayward eyelids rest

Something of old forgotten queens
lurks in the lithe abandon of
your walk

Something of the shackled slave
sobs in the rythm of your talk

Oh! Little brown girl
born for sorrows mate

Keep all that you have of
Queenliness

Forgetting you were once slave
and let your full lips laugh
at Fate!

This is the poem he wrote for "Miss Black America. I once entered this poem in a poetry contest trying to win the grand prize of $1,000.00. It did not win the grand prize, but it did receive an "Honorable Mention". I thought that was pretty cool!

Chapter Four

During the time Tasso spent in New Jersey with his sister, and his enlistment in the Army, he started dating a woman he was introduced to by his sister. Tasso's sister was quite adamant about him dating this woman. He was high and intoxicated during a lot of this time and he didn't remember why he was so willing to comply with his sister's demands. He and the woman ended up getting married! He told me he didn't remember too much about that day and he definitely didn't remember the wedding night! (I once saw a photograph of them on that day, and he did look like he was pretty stoned!) Tasso told me that they did not have too much of a relationship. They never shared a home together, and he really did not see her too much after that day.

This period of Tasso's life was quite difficult for him, as his mother became ill and subsequently died. She passed away on October 14, 1974 (our firstborn child was born on this day in 1978). He returned home to Alabama for her funeral. He was extremely close to his mother. No matter what was going on in his life, he always felt loved, encouraged, and supported by his mother, Ruby, and her death was quite an emotional and traumatic experience for him. (We named our first born daughter after her). After losing him, I can truly understand the hurt and pain he felt when she died!

After Tasso buried his mother, he returned to New Jersey. He spent most of his time smoking weed and drinking alcohol, trying to stay high in an effort to numb the pain he was feeling from the loss of his mother.

He eventually returned to Germany, trying to get back to his normal life and complete his tour of duty in the Army. Shortly after his return, he received a letter from the woman he had married telling him that he was a father. He was shocked and did not think the child could possibly be his due to the timing of the situation. He told me his nephew agreed with him.

By this time, Tasso stated he was unable to function in too much of a normal capacity in the military. He was in constant emotional pain due to the loss of his mother and in constant physical pain from his back injury. Due to the relationship he had established with his commanding officers, he was able to negotiate an early release from his military duties and was granted an honorable discharge from the Army in September, 1975.

Chapter Five

After losing his mother, Tasso was really feeling lost and did not care too much about anything. He stated that he tried to make contact with his wife to determine if he was the father of the child, but she refused to see him or let him see the child. He wanted to establish paternity and be a father to the child, but he was never given the opportunity to do so. Even after the child became of legal age, he tried to establish contact, but was never successful in any of his attempts.

Tasso eventually returned home to Auburn, Alabama, to try and make some sense of his life and gain some direction for the future. Years earlier, his family had been able to move from renting on the sharecropper's land in Loachapoka to buying a home in Auburn. He returned to the family home where his father and two of his brothers were living. One of his mother's brothers had also come to live in Auburn. His uncle was suffering from a genetic, degenerative, neurological disease, and was confined to a wheelchair. He had built a home a couple of doors down from the family home and was living there with Tasso's sister and her children. Tasso spent time at both residences. It was during this transitional moment in Tasso's life that we met again.

Part Two

Cynthia

Chapter Six

I was born on September 15, 1953, in Los Angeles, California, in a home for unwed mothers, where I was to be put up for adoption. My mother was sent there by her parents. You have to understand, this was 1953. Having babies and not being married was taboo back in those days, especially for someone like my mother.

My mother was the second oldest child of five children born to Daniel and Amelia Mitchell. My grandfather was a Porter on the L&N Railway and my grandmother was a stay-at-home Mom and part-time kindergarten teacher. They were upper middle class; high society in the black community. All of the children were college graduates; the only son, a track star; all the girls, debutantes. Girls from this type of family did not have babies out of wedlock; thus the trip to California. The reason I came home to Alabama is a little unclear. I am not sure if my mother saw me and decided to keep me or if her mother, my grandmother, told her to bring me home. At any rate, I was brought home to my grandparents in Montgomery, Alabama.

My mother's best friend, whom I grew up calling "Auntie" (I got my middle name, Jean, from her), says she carried me in her arms all the way from LA to Montgomery. Being a mother myself, I wondered how a new mother could let somebody else hold her baby for what had to be a three or four day trip by train in 1953. It helped me to understand why my mother and I never really had that close mother-daughter type of bond.

She never made that connection with me at birth. I don't think she even held me when I was born, since she was supposed to leave me there. I truly can feel the difference. I love my mother and I think she loved me as best she could, but I was always a living reminder of that time in her life when she "screwed up". At any rate, I began my life living with my mother's parents, Granddaddy and Mama Mitchell.

I was legally adopted by my grandparents in 1959. I did not realize this until I was an adult and needed an official copy of my birth certificate. When I requested it from the State of California, I was informed to contact the Bureau of Vital Statistics in Alabama. My original birth records were sealed by the courts and the only copy of a birth certificate that I could obtain was from Alabama. It shows my grandparents as my parents. To my understanding, no one in my mother's family ever knew who my father was. I think certain people in my mother's family held it against me because my paternity was never revealed to them. I was always Sister's (my mother's family nickname) "illegitimate child"!

My mother introduced me to my father when I was sixteen years old. She and I went to visit a college campus. We spent the day together, shopping and having lunch. We eventually ended up in the office of this biology professor. I was about to graduate from high school and enter college and I thought this was a college campus visit. I was interested in Biology and Chemistry and had very good grades in those subjects. I wanted to pursue a career as a Lab Research Technician. The professor and I had a very interesting conversation about science, careers in the science field, and college classes. All of a sudden, my mother blurted out, "This is your father". I suppose I was in some sort of shock as I just sat there and said nothing. He then asked me, "do you believe her?" He apparently didn't understand how I was raised! I was not about to think or suggest in any way that my Mother might be telling a lie! I answered with, "I don't think she would have waited sixteen years to bring me here to tell me a lie". Of course, I believed her! My mother then asked me to leave the room. I would have loved to have heard that conversation between the two of them!

I think my mother wanted my father and I to develop some sort of a relationship and I would have been okay with that. However, whenever I went to visit him at his office on campus, he always acted like he didn't want anybody to see me there. He was always looking around the corner to make sure no one was in sight! He bought me a couple of gifts, but, I didn't like the fact that he didn't want to be seen with me. I did not appreciate the fact that he was trying to buy me things. I didn't want his gifts! I wanted him to treat me like I was his daughter. He never did! I eventually stopped going to see him.

I don't think his wife ever knew about me. I did not feel it was my place to tell her. That is something the adults should have worked out amongst themselves! As far as I know, he didn't have other children and he never told his wife about me. I understand he died of cancer, but he never contacted me, and never acknowledged me as his child. Even if I didn't want to believe he was my father, genetics don't lie! I looked very much like him. I once saw a picture of him in the University yearbook and my oldest son looks very much like him, as well!

Chapter Seven

My mother went on to teach school in a rural community in Alabama. While there, she fell in love and got married. She and her husband subsequently had four children together. My mother had another child, but like me, she has a father different from our other siblings.

I stayed in the home with my grandparents and I have some fond memories of my childhood there. I remember my grandmother giving me pats of butter when she was in the kitchen cooking. (I love butter to this day). I remember my brother and me playing with the kid next door. He was an only child and must have had every toy known to man! I remember when we used to climb over the chain link fence to go next door to play with him. I remember riding my tricycle outside my grandparent's home. (I am not so sure if this is an actual memory or one I have because I saw a cute picture of me on that tricycle)!

My grandmother suffered a fatal heart attack in 1959. I can't forget her body lying in the coffin in the living room of the family home. At first, everyone was so sad, but then I remember them being so happy. I asked my aunt how that was possible and she told me that was just what people did when someone died. They were sad and cried and then they were happy and laughed. I was confused, as I still felt sad! Nonetheless, my happy days with my grandparents came to an end. I did not deal with the emotion of my grandmother's death until I went to therapy as an adult.

Chapter Eight

I have many fond memories of my childhood growing up in rural Alabama with my new family. Even though everybody knew that I was the "outside" child, no one ever made me feel anything other than loved. Mom's husband was "Daddy" to us all and there was never any "step" anything.

I remember playing outside with my siblings until the street lights came on. We spent time riding bikes, playing ball, and catching lightning bugs. I remember attending church and being a part of the all of the activities children were allowed to participate in.

School was fun, too! When I was five, I went to school with my mother. There were no day care centers (at least not for black children), so I went to school with her. She was the English teacher and school librarian at the school for black people in the next town which was 7 miles away. Her friend was the first grade teacher, and I was supposed to sit in the first grade class and keep quiet and out of the way. However, I was told that I started doing the lessons and participating in class. When it was time for first grade, I had completed all of the first grade work, so I was allowed to enter the second grade at age 6. (That is how I finished high school and was off to college at age 16.)

I remember fun times at school, except I could never get away with anything since my mom was a teacher! I spent some of my elementary school grade years at the local school in our home town and it was fun there, too. I remember walking to and from school with my brother, having fun on the playground, and participating in school programs such as spelling bees, and May Day!

Daddy had his own businesses; a Standard Oil gas station franchise and a barber shop. Mama was teaching school! She and Daddy were happy and seemed to be in love with each other. They were busy with work, kids, and church activities. Life was great!

During Easter weekend and during the summers, I was always sent away to stay with my aunt in Birmingham, Alabama. My aunt and uncle were very good to me and I had lots of fun there! I was able to do lots of things, like participating in the summer reading club at the public library and taking dance, swimming, and typing lessons. I learned how to travel on the city bus by myself. I also remember bowling with my uncle, shopping with my aunt, trips to the zoo, and going to the drive-in movies on those hot and humid summer nights! I worked hard while I was there too! My aunt made sure I had my share of household chores to do! I give her credit for teaching me how to clean today! You had to pass the white glove test in order to be considered eligible for fun and play!

I made friends with the neighborhood kids. One of my summertime friends was one of the girls killed in the infamous Birmingham 16th Street Baptist Church bombing. My aunt and uncle were friends with her parents. Whenever they came to visit, we would always be sent to my room to play and we spent many hours together having fun while the adults socialized.

Imagine the shock of watching TV and seeing her picture on the screen as one of the people killed! I find it strange that no one ever talked to me about losing a friend in such a violent way at such a young age! She was killed on my 10th birthday! I think I remained in shock for many years and did not really mourn her passing until I went to therapy as an adult.

When it was time for school to start and I returned home, I always felt sad when I would hear about all the fun things the family had done while I was away. I would see pictures of trips they had taken to the State park and to the Talladega racetrack and I would always feel so left out! It was like they waited until I was away so they could have fun like a real family!

When my Aunt had her own baby, I no longer spent summers in Birmingham. My summers were then spent in Montgomery, where I was the caretaker of my other aunt's children. I was a teenager by this time. My aunt and her children still lived in the family home with my grandfather. It was great being back in Montgomery! This aunt was the cool aunt and we had much fun staying up nights playing Scrabble, grilling steaks, playing cards, and listening to music! It was like she understood what it was like to be a teenager and we just had fun! This was, of course, on the nights when my grandfather was working and he was away from home! None of that staying up all night and partying was going on when Granddaddy Mitchell was home!

When I would come back home to Ashland, I still felt like an outsider. I was still left out of all the summer family activities. I remember at one point, my mother asked me if I wanted to go and live with my grandfather in Montgomery and finish high school there. One of my aunts that lived there really encouraged me to do so, but I wanted to stay with my mother. Looking back now, I should have realized that my mother probably really wanted me to go live with him. I would have been out of her way. I oftentimes wondered how different my life would have been if I had said yes.

Chapter Nine

Tragedy struck our family in 1964 when our house in Ashland burned completely to the ground! I was told that there was some sort of gas leak from a small space heater in the bathroom. I was in 7th grade by this time. Mama woke me up in the middle of the night, told me to get the baby, go out the front door, and go to our grandmother's house. The family lived on what we would call a city block today, but it was all connected, so it was just across the yard. Remember, this was the era in which children did as they were told, did not talk back, and did not ask questions. It was a good thing I didn't, because by the time I walked around to the front of the house, I could see the entire back of the house in flames! I've told my children and grandchildren this story many times to emphasize the importance of doing what your parents tell you at the time and asking questions later. Had I hesitated that night by asking questions and being hard-headed, we could have all been burned to death!

As you can imagine, this was very hard on my parents as they had lost everything! We ended up moving into our grandmother's house. It was already full as there were four adults and two teen-aged boys already living there. There were six of us in our immediate family at the time, so there were twelve people sharing a 3 bedroom, 1 bath house. My family had been given one bedroom to share, but there was not enough space in the room for me to sleep. At night, I would stay with the family down the road where I shared a room with their daughter. She gave me her clothes to wear and treated me like her little sister. This went on for several months until we eventually moved into a small house across the street while our house was being rebuilt. Things were never the same after the fire!

We eventually moved into our own house again and even though it was new and very nice, things did not get better. There were arguments and fights between my parents. It was clear that things were not going to be peaceful and happy like they were before the fire. Daddy drank constantly and was violent and abusive. His business began to decline and he eventually lost the gas station franchise, closed the barber shop, and took a job at the steel plant in a neighboring town about 20 miles from where we lived.

In 1965, my cousin, a neighborhood friend, and I decided to integrate the all-white school in our town. Integration was coming and we thought we might as well go ahead and get it done! This was quite an experience, as I lived through the Civil Rights Movement right there in that small town in Alabama. We were never on the news and we never had the National Guard to protect us! We were called "nigger", spit on, threatened with hanging and death, and we could not participate in afterschool activities as there was no way they could protect us.

Needless to say, my high school days were not fun! I did, however, learn a lot about white people. It amazed me how at first, they did not want to touch us, treated us like trash, and thought we were stupid. Then, in a few years, when integration became mandatory and they were forced to accept us, they completely changed! By the time graduation came around, they acted like we had been best friends and wanted us to sign yearbooks and trade well wishes! It was like they just forgot how they had initially treated us! I did not forget and was not willing to sweep it under the rug and pretend like none of it ever happened! However, we rocked it academically and put to rest the myth that black kids could not learn and excel in academics! The initial three of us that were there in the first years, all excelled in our studies and we all graduated with honors!

I could not wait to graduate from high school and leave Ashland. Our happy family life was gone, as Daddy continued to drink and became more abusive and violent. I found it hard to keep calling him Daddy, as he was now behaving like a stepfather and treating me like a stepchild. The man who was so loving and kind that I called Daddy was gone when he was drunk. Even now when I speak of him, when I say "Daddy", I am remembering the kind and gentle father. When I call him by his given birth name, I am remembering the abusive and mean alcoholic.

The year I graduated from high school, my mother had another baby which did not belong to her husband. None of us kids knew this at the time, as this type of information was not shared with children. However, I am sure all of the adults in town knew - as it would have been hard to keep something like that a secret in such a small community. When Mom and Dad fought, I would often hear him say things about the man who is my sister's father, but I was young at the time and none of it made any sense to me.

When my mother was pregnant, she shared everything with my little sister and basically shut me out! It was clear the two of them shared a bond that we never had, but one I desperately longed for. I felt so unloved and unwanted! I tried to be the best daughter and big sister that I could be, but there was nothing I could do to make either one of them love me. I did not understand why it was so hard for someone, especially my own mother to love me. I blamed myself for many years for not being good enough or pretty enough or smart enough. Somehow, I thought it was my fault that she didn't love me! I used to stand in my bedroom window and vow that one day I would find somebody to love me, that I would have my own family, and we would be happy! I did not know what I was doing at the time, but I was speaking my life with Tasso into existence. It was many years later, but God gave me exactly the love and the life that I asked for!

I finally graduated from high school and was accepted into Talladega College. I wanted to attend college far away from home, but Mama and I had an agreement; that I would attend the school that offered the best financial aid package. Of course, the school closest to home offered that package. So, off to Talladega College I went! It was only 20 miles away from home. I made another deal with Mama; that we would treat the 20 miles like it was 200. She agreed!

That soon proved to be a mistake for me! One Sunday, I was lonesome and hungry and called home to see what the family was doing. Mama told me she had cooked dinner: cabbage, cornbread, fried chicken, and fried corn. I asked her to bring me a plate. She said she wanted to, but

200 miles was too far to drive just to bring me some food. That was just one of the many times in my life I wished I had kept my mouth shut!

I had not been in college very long when tragedy struck again! This time, my step-father was killed in a head-on car accident! His brother had just died a few days before and the family was still reeling from his death when this terrible accident happened! We were all in a state of shock! It was indeed a very sad and tragic time for the entire family. I was numb, unable to cry or feel anything other than sadness. This is another death, I did not deal with until I went to therapy as an adult.

Chapter Ten

After the funeral, I returned to school to continue with college life. My freshman year, I did very well with my studies. I was quiet, shy, not very outgoing, and spent most of the year just observing everyone and everything. I was really enjoying having my own room and being able to come and go as I pleased.

My sophomore year, I decided to pledge and become a member of Delta Sigma Theta Sorority. That was quite an experience (one I am not so sure I would repeat if I had a do-over). Still, I learned some important life lessons and made some life-long friends. I also learned how to socialize! I learned how to play cards, drink beer, and dance all night! Only thing is, I forgot to go to class! My grades suffered and when I realized I would not graduate with my class, I quickly got my act together. I learned how to go to class, get my work done, and then play cards, drink beer, and dance all night!

I did not have a boyfriend in college, as the guys were not interested in the little skinny girl with the big afro. They were all more into the girls that were more developed than I was. It seems, the guys I did like didn't even know I existed! Most of them treated me like their little sister. It was cool! I was too shy and inexperienced to know what to do anyway! Looking back, it turned out to be kind of a good thing. I say all the time that I can go back to my college reunions, take my husband and kids, and hold my head up because not one guy or girl on campus can tell any stories about how they had me hemmed up in some dorm room or frat house in compromising positions. It never happened!

I ended up changing my major from biology to economics. After my first biology and chemistry lab classes, I realized that high school had not prepared me very well for advanced studies in chemistry and biology and I realized that I knew nothing! I did not think I had what it would take to be a research lab technician. In a way, I fault the college for not paying enough attention to me and realizing that I had entered college at 16 and could have benefitted from some counseling and tutoring. I chose Economics as a major, because it was the only thing left after eliminating everything else I knew I had no interest in! I had to take extra classes every semester in order to earn enough credits to graduate with my class on time. College back in the day was four years; count them: freshman, sophomore, junior, and senior. There were no five year programs unless you were becoming a doctor or a lawyer! I was not about to let my class leave me behind and more importantly, I was not about to let my mother know that I would need extra time to graduate! I did what I had to do, and graduated from Talladega College in May, 1974, with a Bachelor's degree in Economics!

Chapter Eleven

After graduation, I was home in Ashland for two days, when my mother asked what my plans were. I had no intention of staying in Ashland, but I had not yet formulated a plan of action. After being prompted to make a move, I packed my belongings, counted my graduation money ($200), and headed off to Atlanta, Georgia, in my canary yellow Chevy Malibu, to seek my fame and fortune. Atlanta was the place to be at the time, as black people were able to find jobs and be successful if they had a college degree.

I first came to East Point where two of my male cousins had an apartment. I didn't have any place of my own to stay, so sometimes I would go to their apartment to shower and change clothes. A female cousin had just graduated from Emory University and had a few weeks left on her lease. She told me I could stay there for a few weeks until the lease was up. I would go there sometimes and spend the night. However, she shared the apartment with a couple of white girls and they had a bird! I did not like white people or birds, so I did not go there very often! Most of the time, I would park outside my cousin's apartment in East Point and sleep in my car.

I finally found a job as a typist in the mail room at the executive office for the Days Inn motel chain. I made $500.00 a month (before taxes). Somehow, I managed to save enough money and got my first apartment in Stonetree Apartments in East Point. It was a proud and happy day when I moved in with only my purse, my pillow and blanket, my clothes, my record player, and my albums!

Money was tight, but I was on my way! I eventually saved up enough money to buy a bed, then a small black and white TV, then a dining room table and chairs! I was living the life! I barely had enough money to pay rent, car note, and keep the lights on – food was optional! I remember my fellow Talladega classmate was living with her sister in the same apartment complex. She was unemployed and looking for a job. We used to get one meal at Church's Chicken; two wings and a biscuit for $.89 and a large soda for $.79. We would each get a wing, cut the biscuit in half, divide the soda and that was dinner!

I was doing several jobs at the Days Inn executive offices outside of my own tasks, from working the switchboard, helping deliver and process the mail, and typing letters for the Personnel Director's secretary! When I asked about an increase in pay for all the extra work I was doing, I was told that people working in the mail room were not eligible for raises! I knew then that I had to make a move! My college classmate told me about an ad she had seen in the newspaper where Eastern Airlines was hiring flight attendants. There was paid training, the opportunity to travel, and the pay was way more money than I was making at my office job. I took a day off work and we both went to apply. They called us both back for a second, then a third interview. At the third interview, they offered me the job, but not her!

I felt really bad as she was the one who had told me about the job in the first place. However, everything worked out as it was supposed to. She ended up moving to Chicago for a better job opportunity, met her husband, and eventually ended up in California, where she and her hubby happily reside today! She has been a good friend throughout the years and we still keep in touch!

Chapter Twelve

Being a flight attendant for a major airline was a great experience! I left Atlanta for six weeks of training in Miami, Florida, on January 1, 1975. Training was hard work and there was lots of studying and testing crammed into a few short weeks. There were about eight black people in my training class and we were all coming back to be based in Atlanta! That worked out great for me since I already had an apartment close to the airport!

It was great to be in Miami in January! I had never been in such a warm climate in the winter and quite frankly did not believe it could be true. I carried my leather coat with me to Miami thinking it could not possibly be that warm. It was winter after all! However, it was 80 degrees and sunshine nearly every day! That coat hung in the closet until it was time to return to Atlanta. It was quite a shock to come back to the cold rainy weather in Atlanta in February. I was beginning to wish I had requested Miami as a home base!

I settled into life as a flight attendant! I was on call four days a week and off for three days. When on call, you had to be by the phone and able to get to the airport within 45 minutes. There were no cell phones. There were pagers, but I couldn't afford one at the time! The phone company had a service where you could transfer your calls to another person's home phone and sometimes my friends and I would do that so we could get together and wait to see who would get a call to go to work! There were times when you would get a call to go, and times when you didn't! It was exciting to pack a bag and fly off to destinations unknown (until you got to the airport) at the last minute!

My friends and I were all single, and we spent our off days, shopping, traveling, and going to our favorite nightclub on Campbellton Road for "Happy Hour". We were on call and working on the weekends so our off days were mostly weekdays. During "Happy Hour", the drinks were two for one, and we would have the club mostly to ourselves as most people had to be at work during the time when we were off. We would have our fun and be out before the "club crazies" would come in! I think that kept us out of a lot of trouble!

The dating scene in Atlanta was quite a mess at the time. Atlanta was known as the "single man's paradise". There were supposedly fifteen women to every one man and the men had the women in competition to see which one was going to provide the most "amenities" for him. That was not my game! I was not looking for anyone to take care of and I was certainly not going to compete with other women for a man! I had low self-esteem. I was skinny, shy, and did not see myself being able to compete with the more attractive, more physically endowed women. I had decided that I would focus on traveling and would enjoy my life the way it was. Little did I know what was just around the corner for me!

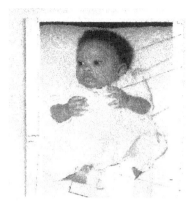

My baby photo

On my tricycle- age three

Elementary School Days

Summer in Birmingham

Talladega College Graduation Day

Flight Attendant Days

[57]

Part Three

The Beginning...

Chapter Thirteen

I first met Tasso when I was only 14 years old. It was during our school spring break when I was visiting my first cousin in Auburn, Alabama. Her father and my mother were siblings and we were the first grandchildren in the Mitchell family. Even though her parents were divorced, our families made sure that we kept in touch with each other. My Uncle and Aunt were both teachers at Drake High School and Tasso had been a student in both of their classes. Tasso was the star player of the Drake High School basketball team where he was known to average 26 points or more a game! Of course, all the local girls had a crush on him and I'm sure my cousin was no exception! She was very excited that he had come for a visit! I had been told that he was somewhat quiet and shy and in spite of the all the local girls who deemed themselves in love with him, he did not have a girlfriend at the time.

I remember that day clearly. He was sitting on the piano stool, arms crossed, with one hand under his chin. My cousin and I were standing there side by side holding hands. She was grinning and looking silly. I was too shy to even smile (especially with my aunt standing directly behind us). Apparently, I did not understand the magnitude of this visit! He did not say much and he did not stay long. He told me years later after we had become a couple, that he knew that day that our paths would cross again, but he would have to wait for me to grow up. There was a four year age difference. I was just beginning high school and he was about to graduate from high school and head off to college.

Chapter Fourteen

Over the years, as I communicated with my cousin, I always kept up with all the people who I had met on my visits to her hometown. Tasso was one of those people. I knew that he had graduated from high school and had gone on to Tougaloo College in Tougaloo, Mississippi, on a basketball scholarship.

Early in the summer of 1970, after my high school graduation and as I was preparing for college, a friend of Tasso's came to my hometown to visit someone he knew. He stopped by to see me and told me that he had been instructed to give me Tasso's home address. He made it clear to me that Tasso expected me to write to him. Apparently, I did, because in August of 1970, I received a letter from Tasso. It was clear in his letter that he was responding to something I had written to him. He wrote to me from Newark, New Jersey, where he was staying after spending the summer in Boston, Massachusetts. He told me all about his plans for the rest of the summer before returning to Tougaloo for what must have been his senior year. I was so quiet that day (I never uttered one word) when he visited my cousin's house. I was really surprised that he had even paid any attention to me at all. I am even more surprised that I had the nerve to write to him.

When you read his letter to me, you will understand why I feel that he knew that our paths would cross again in the future. There are just subtle hints; like he knew I would choose Talladega College, he liked my name, he was glad I liked his, made sure I knew where to write to him in the future, and above all he signed the letter "yours truly". Hmmmm…..

It is a mystery to me as to how I was able to retain possession of this letter. So many of my keepsakes, yearbooks, and other mementos from my high school and college days that were left at my mother's house were destroyed and I am not quite sure how this letter survived. But, yet it did!

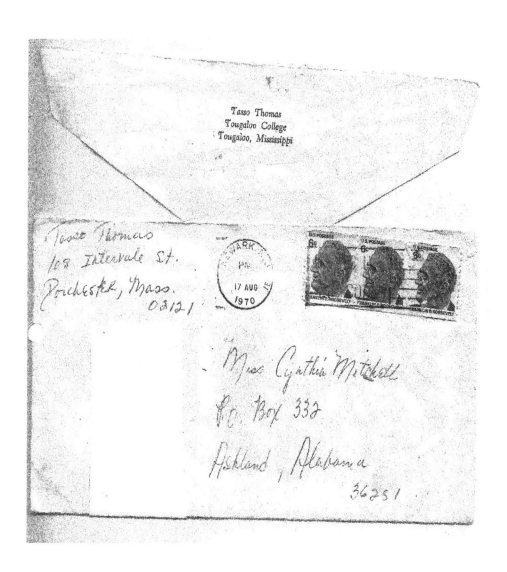

Tasso Thomas
Tougaloo College
Tougaloo, Mississippi

Tasso Thomas
108 Intervale St.
Dorchester, Mass.
02121

Miss Cynthia Mitchell
P.O. Box 332
Ashland, Alabama
36251

Hi Cynthia,

Today is another one of those days—
Pull—dead and dreary—

So you want to know about
Boston—Well let me tell you about Boston—It ain't shit—pardon
the expression—But that's the only
way I can describe it—Of Course there are a lot of happenings
For instance since I've been
here there have been many shows.
This night Club—The Sugar Shack
has the best in the business
down every week—The Five
Stair Steps and Cubie—The Funk-
adelics—Little Anthony and the
Imperials—The Dells—The Parli-
ments and etc. have all been in
town since I've been here,

II

at the present _Watts 103 st Rythm band is down_. Oh yea!
They have a big thing out to
Harvard Stadium every week.
It's really a summer Festival.
~~the~~ Supremes were out monday
night. Ike and Tina Turner was
there week before last – As you
can see there are plenty of
happenings in Boston. But the
happenings (don't) aren't really
happenings if you don't have
someone – to make the happenings
with. (dig!)

    I'm glad you like my name
– why. because I like it. (smile)
About my job – It's over – I have
gave it up – I feel that I have
ploved enough this summer –

II

For the next two weeks I will
be travelling. Frist I'm going to
Newark, N.J. — which isn't but
about 300 miles from here. After
that I'll proably go out west.
Tell you what I'll send you a
post Card of each place — O.K. O.K.
   Atlanta is a real hip place — If
you don't already know (smile) — you'll
dig it —
   Sorry that you couldn't (didn't)
make it to Detroit — maybe later
on in life, huh!
   Gonzaloo is A real hip school
and I could dig your coming
if you decide against 'dega ....
more than likely you will de
cide on 'dega.
   Oh yea! I know Eddie — pretty
hip dude.... you proably found

[68]

IV

that to be true from the time he
was in Ashland. Right! Right!
Hey, I'm writing you just the
cold - as if I really know you -
Let's say that I do and let it
go at that - Al-right.....

Cynthia - very cute name ---- I
like it - And that's saying a lot -
since it's coming from me.... (smile)

About answering my letter - write
when you write - elf it's within
the next week or so - before the
'30th of Aug. Address it to my home
address ....

      1034 ZELLARS AVE.
      Auburn, Alabama
        36830

P.s. Take Care   yours Truly
Let me hear from   Tosso
you (soon)

Part Four

"We" began...

May 31, 1976

Chapter Fifteen

The next time I heard from Tasso was May 31, 1976. My two best friends and I had just returned from a trip to Bermuda the day before. It was Memorial Day weekend and I still had a few days off and anticipated attending some party or barbecue before returning to work. Everybody I called already had plans and they did not include me! I decided I would go and visit my former college roommate and her husband in Chicago. I had some housekeeping and laundry I needed to do so I decided I would take care of those chores and take a "red eye" (late night) flight to O'Hare.

Before I could finalize those plans, I got a phone call from Tasso. He stated he had run into my cousin in Auburn and she told him I was a flight attendant living in Atlanta. My cousin gave him my phone number and suggested he give me a call. Tasso said he had planned to be in Atlanta later that day and he asked if he could come by for a visit around noon. I said, "Yes".

I don't know why I agreed to let him come to my apartment. I wanted to see him, but I was a single woman living alone in a big city and I never let men come to my apartment! A girl had to be careful! Yet, I did not give it a second thought. Maybe I felt comfortable since he was someone I had met before. Little did I know that my entire life was about to change!

As it approached noon, I was not quite done with my laundry. I lived around the corner from the laundromat so I ran back home and left a note on my door letting him know I would be right back . I did not want to miss his visit! As it turned out, I had time to finish the laundry, get back home, shower, and change clothes before he arrived.

He knocked on the door and when I opened it, I felt this force pushing me towards him. I felt like I was supposed to grab him and give him a big hug! I didn't, however, because I didn't want him to think I was some sort of aggressive, crazy chick. I just stood there holding onto the door for dear life! He was standing outside, looking quite dazed, as if he wasn't sure whether or not he was in the right place. He started explaining how he had parked his car in the wrong spot, kept looking around like he had lost something, and he needed to go move the car. I said, okay, but, I did notice that the car was only a couple of spaces down from my apartment. At any rate, he moved the car up a couple of spaces and came inside. I attributed his confused, dazed look to the heat!

You have to understand, it was a typical hot, muggy, southern summer day! Even though it was technically still spring, it was one of those days where you could step outside and break a serious sweat just walking to your car! The thermometer may have said 85 degrees, but it felt more like 95! Anyone who has lived in the South or visited in the summertime knows exactly what I mean!

Tasso and I had been together over 10 years when we were talking one night and I told him about the force I felt that day when I opened the door. He told me he had felt the same thing! He said he didn't want to just grab me as he didn't want me to get the wrong idea about him! That

[74]

explained the dazed state he appeared to be in! Talk about the forces of nature at work!

We spent the next few minutes making polite conversation. Tasso said he was hungry and asked about something to eat. I traveled for a living and did very little cooking, so cereal, milk, and a couple of eggs were about all I had in the fridge. We decided to go out for a bite to eat and ended up at the Waffle House on Washington Road. He began sharing knowledge on that very day as he made sure the waitress knew that he didn't eat pork and gave her very specific instructions as to how his food was to be prepared. I had not eaten pork in quite a while as I had only recently recovered from food poisoning from eating a ham and cheese sandwich in Buffalo, New York! When he began to explain why he did not eat pork, it led to a very interesting discussion on several other topics. I remember thinking, nice-looking, intelligent, and he has not even asked what I was going to do for him! Wow, this is different!

After our meal, we ended up spending the entire day together. We went downtown to Peaches Records and Tapes. Long playing albums were in then (this was after cassette tapes and before CD's). It was a huge record warehouse where you could find almost every album known to man! It was the 70's and there was no shortage of great music from great artists; many of whom we still listen to today. He purchased several albums: The Isley Brothers, The O'Jays, Chaka Khan, and Sly and the Family Stone to name a few! It was my first introduction to what we call "smooth jazz" today, as he also bought albums by Donald Byrd and the Blackbyrds, Jean Carn, Natalie Cole and several others.

When we left the record store, we ended up in Piedmont Park. Someone took pictures of us in the park that day (without us knowing) and I have those photos today in a frame, entitled "Our Day". To me they document the beginning of our lives together, as we were truly joined together that day in mind, body, and spirit! Those photos depict our whirlwind meeting, dating, proposal, acceptance, wedding, and reception.....all on our day, May 31, 1976! Of course, we were still unaware that all of this was happening! (The last two photos of the series were taken back at my apartment later that evening).

It has only been in recent years that I learned the significance of our being in Piedmont Park. The term *piedmont* is a specific geographical term; a plateau where certain areas of land converge. We were in a specific place on earth that signified the joining of land; we were joining our lives, minds, and spirits together in that spot on earth without even being consciously aware that it was even happening! This further lends proof to the fact that the forces of the universe were in perfect alignment on that day and we were destined to be in this life together! What God brought together, no man can tear apart!

As evening approached, we left the park, stopped and bought some beer, and headed back to my apartment. We began to listen to some of the records he bought that day; just chilling and enjoying the music. It was so hot and muggy and we had been out in the heat all day, so Tasso asked if he could take a shower. Of course, I allowed him. I directed him to the bathroom, gave him some towels, and proceeded to chill some glasses for us to enjoy a really cold beer when he finished. But then, he came out of the shower…

I could not help but notice his hair: jet black, wet, and curly, the water glistening off of his broad shoulders, his narrow waist, and slightly bowed legs. *Wow…* was all I could think. (I recently saw a picture of a famous athlete on the cover of a magazine as he was coming up out of a pool of water wearing only his boxing shorts. The photo reminded me of how Tasso looked when he came out of the shower that day. I have that magazine cover framed on my bedroom wall!) I offered him a cold glass of beer and as he turned to walk back to the living room, I took a towel and dried off his back. (He later told me that he thought that was such a sweet and caring gesture and my touch sent chills down his spine!). A sistah just wanted to touch the brotha and make sure he was real! Soon after, I decided to take a shower, too!

When I came out of the shower, he was sitting on the side of the bed, with his towel around his waist. I was wrapped in my towel and had every intention of going to my closet for something sexy to wear, but I had to pass by the bed to get to the closet. I never made it. I walked right up to him, like I was magnetically drawn to him, the towel came off, and the rest you could say was the first night of the rest of my life!

I cannot stress how out of character this was for me. First of all, I **never** took anyone to my apartment. I **never** had sex on the first date. Hell,

[77]

I barely had sex with anyone at all even on the second or third date for that matter. It was as if I was not operating on my own. I was under some sort of spell and I had no control! Looking back, I realize that I was not in control! We were brought together by a divine force that was greater than the two of us! Neither one of us expected anything like this to happen!

Tasso told me that night that he loved me. I asked him how he could possibly know that when we had just met. He said we had not just met and that he just knew. I told him it wasn't necessary to use the word "love". I told him that I knew that is just what guys say when they want to get you into bed. He had already gotten me there, so he don't have to say that. Well, he told me he loved me and that's all there was too it!

We spent the night together, listening to the Isley Brothers "Harvest for the World", making love, and just being together... just feeling... not speaking... just being in the moment. It was truly one of the most romantic experiences of my life!

The next morning, I expected him to get dressed, say goodbye/see you later, and whatever. He did just the opposite! He kept saying he had to go, but he never made a move towards the door. We were sitting at my kitchen table. I was sitting on his lap and every time he said he had to go, I would try to get up, but he kept holding me and wouldn't let me go! After about 30 minutes or so of this, I told him I still had a few days off. I could follow him to Alabama and we could spend a little more time together. He agreed! He let me go; I grabbed a change of clothes, and followed him back to Auburn.

We got a room at the Auburn Inn in downtown Auburn where we spent another magical night together! I had never experienced sex with anyone the way I did with Tasso and we could not get enough of each other! We created some magic together which continued for 37 years! Being with him is one of the many things I miss and I cannot even imagine being with another man the way I was with him. I have said that whatever pleasures God intended for a man and woman to experience together through sex, Tasso and I experienced all of those pleasures. I will be forever grateful that God allowed me to experience such deep physical and emotional love with a man as wonderful as Tasso!

When we finally had to part ways, I was close to my hometown of Ashland and decided to stop in for a quick visit before returning to Atlanta. When I walked in the door, my mother took one look at me and asked, "What's his name?" I pretended not to know what she meant as I was not ready to share the joy of my new found love with anyone. I guess there really is such a thing as "the look of love" and I guess I had it!

By the time I returned to Atlanta, I received a letter from Tasso. In that letter, he expressed his feelings for me in a poem entitled, "Perceptions". I say all the time that I must have been a "super bad chick", because in just three days I went from being "Cynthia" to "Baby"!

I had to go back to work on a three-day trip, and I took that letter with me. I could barely focus on what I was doing or where I was going, because all I wanted to do was read my poem. I read it over and over again until I memorized every single word! No one had ever told me they loved me before (well, okay, maybe somebody had), but nobody ever backed it up with words and actions! No one had ever taken the time to express their feelings and emotions in such a beautiful way. Looking back now, I can see that the poem was my proposal. He was offering me his love and a whole new life that he and I could share… and I wholeheartedly accepted!

Tasso also wrote several other poems for me in the early days of our relationship. He would give them to me when I would come home from a long trip. He wanted me to understand how he felt about me and how much he missed me when I was away. I thought they were beautiful and I was so honored that he cared enough about me to put his feelings into words. His poems, cards, and letters are among my most prized possessions.

3 June '76

Hi Baby,

It's Thursday afternoon and I just left the Gym. I showed my _ass_ on those white boys (smile). It's now about 7:30 and my nephew is playing a ball-game. He's the star pitcher and they're playing for 1st place in there division. Today before I went to the gym I took my uncle to Montgomery to see his X wife — Man was that a trip. (smile)

Oh yea! The poem that you are about to read, or get into came about as a result of me trying to understand my emotions and wanting you to understand. Since you been gone I've been missing you so damn much until it hurts. I wish you were around all the time — so you could feel what I mean.

Sage...

Common sage (salvia officinalis) has historically been the herb of health and of the aged. It has been used to help nerves, cure palsy and fever, for headaches, to strengthen gums, whiten teeth, and as a wash to darken grey hair. Cut leaves of common sage for cheese sandwiches, souffles, and stuffings. Use dried in sausages, with cheese, pork, poultry, as stuffing seasoning in turkey, and as a tea.

Perceptions:

At best you are the sus-
taining force in my life.
All around me there are
allusions.
People living in confusion.
Happy to see your face
today
'cause love you see don't
come easy
At times it seems you
are but a dream
but when you smile
it makes me know
love is here and life
is for you and I
              to share
                    to live

this old world is con-
stantly changing,
    all the time
              rearranging

Living is hard
                and sometimes
we reach out for a
    helping hand
all alone
        and never caring
fantling, no end to the
fantasies
won't you come with me
love of mine
I'll show you a world of
a different kind
Always at the end
                of a dreary
                    day
we find no solitude
in a lie
cause the truth you see
is only in the believer

[83]

won't you come
with me
love of mine
I'll show you, a world
of a different kind

always I know
you'll give
all the love I need
all the love I need
please come with me
my little Angel
come with me
stay, please stay,
always
in a world of a different
kind ----

You see Cynthia, I have found my center—my own center—inside myself. And it shows. And that's a crime in this country to be free, even within your own self. I'm glad I found you cause you see I know you're free too!

P.S. I miss you!

Love—
"Pure J"

The Meeting

The Date

The Proposal

The Answer

The Wedding

The Reception

Outside the apartment at Stonetree

Enjoying listening to music

[87]

Something moves within
every time you touch me

And I love the way you
touch me

won't you touch me
one more time

The way you touched me first
time ever we met
The way you touched me last
your eyes are so revealing
this feeling I'll always be gaining
like nature gives so that we
can live
Once I feared the inevitable
no more 'cause now you're here
giving me all I could ever
want - to live

Something grows within everytime
you touch me

[88]

And I love the feeling

So won't you touch me
one more time
the way you touched me
last time last time we made
love

It's only you – you my dear –
are the only one
I give my love too

I wish you were here with me
tonight to love me

Over and over again

you see my love – this love inside
for you there's no end......

[89]

Songs are about love
Songs are about people
Songs are about people in love

Singing is about feelings
feelings are about the inner self

Being complete is about being
in harmony with the universe

Songs are about Completeness
about being one with another
Love is about understanding
Love is understanding

to understand is to be a very
wise man

I think that I am a very
lucky man, "I got you."

[90]

Chapter Sixteen

Over the next several weeks, we were together whenever I was free. I was working a three day on, four day off schedule, and Tasso always knew when I would be coming back from a trip. Either I would come home and go to Auburn, or I would get home and he would come to Atlanta. It was clear that we had started something and neither one of us was interested in letting go. As more time passed, he just began to stay in Atlanta. He began to feel uncomfortable in my one bedroom flat; everything there belonged to me. He said if we were going to be together, we needed to be someplace that was ours. When my lease was up, we moved into a two bedroom townhouse in Club Candlewood on Washington Road, still in East Point.

Shortly before we moved in together, I went to Auburn to visit Tasso and we met at our usual place, The Holiday Inn, at the Tuskegee exit. He hesitated before he went inside to secure a room and seemed to be quite upset about something. He told me he had to tell me something before we could continue. This was the night he told me about his "marriage". He knew that I was really particular about truth and honesty, and he felt he had to let me know that he was legally married. He said that he was afraid I would no longer want to be with him. He did not consider himself to be in a marriage other than legally. I did not care... I loved him, he loved me, and I was not about to let some past mistake interfere with what we had! I always said I never would date a married man, but I guess

I did. I let him go ahead and get the room that night. I guess I have to add that to the list of things I have to ask God to forgive me for.

We moved into our new apartment, furnished it, and went about the business of living together as a couple. I was his and he was mine. He always stated that he did not need a license from the "white man" giving him permission to declare me as his. I did not have a problem with that. We were both very "pro-black". It was more important to me that we were committed in our heart, minds, and bodies and his argument about not needing the white man's permission or approval was fine with me.

We spent our time traveling, watching sports (he patiently taught me everything about football that I had never understood), enjoying great sex, and good food. He always had a healthy appetite. We spent many hours in long philosophical discussions about life and the things we both wanted to achieve. We had a lot in common as far as long term goals. Tasso always had an entrepreneurial mindset. He was also a Muslim and he began teaching me about Islam and the Quran. I didn't just take Tasso's word for it. I did my own studying and research. It was the first time a religion and its principles made sense to me and how I wanted to live my life. I guess you could say I converted to Islam.

My family thought I was losing my mind and that I was letting this man lead me down the path straight to hell and self-destruction. What my family thought about me was the least of my concerns. They had never had too much positive to say about anything I did, anyway. His family did not express much love for me either. I suppose they saw me as some sort of threat; I was taking their brother away from them. We wanted both of our families to love us as much as we loved each other, but it was clear to us very early on that it was not going to happen. We were on our own! It didn't matter to either one of us. We were in love and committed to being together.

Don't misunderstand. Our relationship was not without its flaws. In fact, it was far from it! I had never been in a relationship like this before, and from all the love that was being shared between the two of us, I always expected complete honesty and fidelity. Tasso was conflicted as it appeared that he was dating someone else before he met me and it seemed that he was trying to decide who would work out best for him. He would leave the apartment, take my car, say he was going to the store, and show up two days later. I would be hurt, angry, and worried. You name the emotion, I had it! I didn't know if he had been hurt in an accident or if he had just decided to leave me. I would be equally upset because he left me stranded without MY car! I already suffered with low self-esteem and would not have been surprised if he had found someone else who he thought was better for him than me. Whenever he would come back, I would make it perfectly clear that I would not let him continue to treat me that way and that if that is how it was going to be, we could call it quits! I was not willing to be in a relationship and be second fiddle to anyone or continue to be hurt in this way!

I know, I know… I should have kicked him to the curb the first time it happened. My logical mind wanted me to, but he would apologize to me, always have a good explanation for his behavior, back it up with some mind-blowing, extra good loving, and that was the end of it! I guess he eventually made up his mind, as it stopped happening and all was good!

In January 1978, I became pregnant. His first response was "I guess we'll have to get married". I was the first to say, "Whoa, wait, not so fast!" I wanted to be with him, but I never wanted him to feel like he HAD to marry me or that I got pregnant to "keep him" with me. It was quite the opposite. I was in the 1% group of people who became pregnant while on the pill. I told him that marriage under this condition would not be necessary, if and when we legally married, it would be because it is something we both wanted, not because of a baby! We continued on with our lives as usual. In reality, I should have said, "yes, absolutely" and marched on down to the courthouse, but as they say, hindsight is 20/20.

In the first few months of pregnancy, I had extreme morning, afternoon, and evening nausea and it was difficult for me to continue flying. I was worried about what effect the strenuous rigors of flying would have on the baby, so I went on early maternity leave after about 3 months. Tasso did not have much success in the Atlanta job market, and he had decided to go into business in Alabama with his uncle. They had invested in a restaurant and nightclub outside of Auburn and he would have to be there full-time to get everything going. I decided to go with him. I did not want to be pregnant and alone in Atlanta, and if we were going to be a family and raise a child we needed to be together. We packed up our belongings and moved to his uncle's house in Auburn. It wouldn't take long for me to find out that this was not a good idea!

It was difficult not to have our own space. Tasso's sister and her children lived in the home with his uncle and they were not very nice to me. I felt uncomfortable and was only happy when Tasso was there. I thought things might improve when I met his other sister from New Jersey. Tasso had always spoken so highly of her and I thought I finally would meet someone who was a little more intelligent and who would be willing to get to know me, but, boy was I wrong! I guess the saying, "blood is thicker than mud", holds true! She stood back on those long legs and looked down her nose at me, and that was it. I was officially gum on the bottom of the shoe! My being pregnant didn't help! They even made references to the child not being Tasso's (of course, none of those comments were ever made where Tasso could hear them)!

At any rate, the nightclub venture turned out to be a nightmare! It was doomed before it started! It was supposed to be a family-operated business, but the only thing the family did was eat up all the food, feed their friends, drink up all the beer, and give nothing in return. It was not long, before the operation was in the red, and they had no choice but to close down.

Tasso and I returned to Atlanta with nothing, as everything we owned had been "disposed of" by his family. Neither of us wanted to bring a baby into the world under these conditions, so we felt it best to start over. We struggled over the next few months, unable to keep a place of our own due to the lack of finances. We eventually ended up staying with his nephew who had moved to Atlanta from New Jersey. His nephew and his girlfriend were happy to share their apartment with us. That worked out fine for a while, except, his nephew was into some things that were not quite legal, and after a drive-by shooting at the apartment one night, Tasso decided it was no longer safe for me to be there. I moved in with my flight attendant friend who lived in an apartment complex across the street. Tasso remained in the apartment with his nephew.

On October 14, 1978, we became parents to our son, Tasso Ashuntu, who was born on the same day that Tasso's mother had passed away (years earlier). Tasso was thrilled to be a father! My friend was gracious enough to accommodate us during those first few weeks that I was out of the hospital. I eventually returned to work, we got our own place, and proceeded to return to our lives, only now we had a baby!

We struggled as Tasso was still trying to find a traditional job and come up with ways he could start his own business. It was hard being a flight attendant with no family support. I worked turn-arounds (day trips) for the first few months back. I would have a 3:00 am check-in, fly from Atlanta, to Raleigh, to D.C., then New York, reverse the route, and return home around noon. I would need to sleep, but couldn't, as I had a baby to take care of! We did the best we could. I eventually got outbid on the turn-around day trips and had to fly two and three day trips where I would be gone for one or two nights. That made things even more difficult! Both our families claimed they would help us out, but we soon would find out we could trust neither side to live up to their word.

My mother offered to help, but the first weekend I needed to leave my baby there, she ended up being angry with me for some reason. I still to this day do not understand why. She verbally and physically attacked me. Tasso did not interfere, until she grabbed our son. She ended up attacking him and biting him on the arm. (He went to his grave with the scar from that bite on his arm.) Needless to say, we left there running for our lives in the middle of the night! In spite of that outburst, Tasso never ever uttered a single disrespectful word towards my mother or anyone in my family. Just the opposite, he always encouraged me to communicate and keep in touch with them. He assured me one day, that it would all be okay. He was right, but I was so hurt. I just couldn't see it at the time.

When we left my mother's house that night, we ended up in Loachapoka at the home of one of Tasso's Muslim brothers. He and his wife were more than kind and gracious and shared their home with us for several months. They treated us with more love and respect than we had received from any member of our families. I learned how to cook while I was in their home! I watched his wife make whole wheat cornbread, cook lentils, and filet fish. I have passed that whole wheat cornbread recipe down to my children. It is the only cornbread they know!

His wife helped us with babysitting while I continued to travel back and forth to Atlanta to continue working. I am forever grateful for the love and kindness they showed us!

[97]

Whenever we left the baby with Tasso's family in Auburn, I would come in from a trip and find him left at home with his teenaged niece; no adult in sight, with a snotty nose, dirty diaper, and... you get the drift! It was unacceptable! I would always be angry with Tasso, because he was supposed to be there with him. I always wanted to be a good parent. For better or worse, I wanted to raise my child. I took my responsibility as a parent very seriously. I decided I could not be the best parent for my child while traveling for a living, so I decided to leave my job at Eastern Airlines. I did not think ahead to what this would mean financially. I just knew I had to try my best to be a good mother to my son. I owed him that!

We decided to live in Montgomery, Alabama. It was close to his hometown of Auburn, without being in Auburn, and we both thought job opportunities would be better for Tasso there. Wrong! He was not able to find work. We eventually lost our apartment and ended up moving back to Auburn with his family.

Tasso started a business with a friend of his in Tuskegee who was a gifted and talented furniture designer. He built and designed these beautiful portable beverage bars and Tasso was the salesman. I handled all the paperwork and office duties. The problem was that Tasso could sell the items; people wanted them, companies wanted to sell them in their stores and they were willing to pay a hefty price for them, but, our builder could not or would not build them in a timely fashion. I understood being a creative genius and all, but he did not understand the concept of a deadline! When Tasso could not deliver the goods as promised, you know what happened – another business venture down the tubes and no money to show for it!

By this time, it was 1982 and we were living back in the family home in Auburn. Tasso's father became ill and died. I became pregnant with our second child. Our daughter, Ruby (named after Tasso's mother) was born in May of that year. Once again, Tasso was so excited to be a dad! When Ruby was a few months old, my mother came to Auburn to visit and wanted me to come and stay at home in Ashland for a while. I guess she knew I was not really comfortable being with Tasso's family. Even with a new baby, my presence was barely tolerated! I agreed to go home with my mother as it would give me some relief and it would give Tasso time to get things together so we could have our own place again. I always supported Tasso in his business ventures and his desire to be his own boss. He had such vision and such passion, and it was easy to imagine that the things he wanted to do were possible. He believed in his abilities and I believed in him! I knew that he would eventually find the right business and he would be successful!

Living in Ashland, was cool for a while. I never at any time intended to live there on a permanent basis. I had been so unhappy growing up there and there was nothing to do except work at the chicken plant or sewing factory. These were not options for a college graduate! Tasso and I both knew that what we were going through was only temporary! We were willing to make a few sacrifices for a bigger reward in the long run.

I loved Tasso very much and I had no intentions of being a single parent or being away from the man I loved or the father of my children for too long. My sister was living at home with her two children and I thought it was cool. We would get a chance to bond as mothers, sisters, and adults. However, problems began to surface. My mother became irritated with me and she would come home from work angry and blame everything that went wrong (or not wrong) on me! I did not understand until years later where all of this was coming from (another story for another time), but at any rate, I knew I could no longer continue to stay in her home under such conditions. Tasso had a childhood friend who he had introduced me to months earlier that lived in Talladega, Alabama, with his wife and children. When I told Tasso that the kids and I could no longer stay in Ashland, he made arrangements for his friend to help me get back to him in Tuskegee.

I arranged for a ride to Talladega one morning with a relative who worked there and he took me to the home of Tasso's friend. Tasso's friend and his wife treated the kids and I like royalty. They made sure we were comfortable, had plenty to eat, and paid for our bus ticket later that evening so we could get back to Tasso. I will never forget their hospitality, generosity, and kindness. As I boarded the bus that afternoon, my mother came on board and asked me why I was leaving. I don't know why she didn't understand just how unhappy we were living there. There was no time to explain. I just told her my children and I had to go home. Tasso did not even have a place for us to live. We stayed with a distant cousin of his for a few weeks until we got an apartment in Auburn and began to resume our lives again!

Things were looking up! Tasso had teamed up with a couple of his Muslim brothers and they had started a business. They would buy clothing, jewelry, etc. at wholesale prices and go out on the road to small towns in various parts of Alabama and sell them to the public. They were quite successful! They would leave home on Thursday with a van full of goods, and come back on Sunday with a pocket full of cash! Even though the money was good, Tasso knew he wanted more for himself and his family.

It was late 1982 and I became pregnant again! I was shocked! How could this be happening to me! Ruby was only 6 months old! Once again, I seemed to be a candidate for being in the 1% group of another failed method of birth control. This time, I was pregnant with twins!!! Tasso was always so excited to become a dad, but this time I think he was just a little bit nervous! When I told him we would be having two babies at once, he just got up, said he was going to work, and left. He was gone for a couple of days and I was worried that he might not come back! He did, and all was well! We welcomed our fraternal twins, Jamaal and Jamilah, into the world in August of 1983!

It was an exciting time for us! We went from having two kids, to having four! It really got real for us! Tasso was excited, as usual, to be a dad again! He was really feeling super bad at this time, now that he had made two babies at once! Whatever! Even though things had begun to improve for us financially, Tasso and I decided that we would move back to Atlanta. There were limited opportunities in Auburn and Tasso never wanted to raise his family there anyway. We were going to wait until I recovered from the birth of the twins and we were headed back to Atlanta!

In October 1983, tragedy struck! The twins were eight weeks old and I was just beginning to recover from my childbirth ordeal (I had delivered two babies that weighed almost 7 pounds each) when my mother was involved in a near-fatal accident. She was hit head-on by a tractor-trailer truck! She had been airlifted to a hospital in Birmingham. Tasso and I packed up the kids and went to be by her side. My cousin, who lived in Birmingham at the time, was gracious enough to offer us a place to stay so I could be at my mother's bedside for a few days. Mama was in a coma and they were not sure if she would ever wake up. I knew I could not remain at my cousin's home indefinitely, so we decided that I would go the family home in Ashland and stay until we could determine what would happen with my mother.

I was trying to offer help the best way I could at the time. I had four children, Ashuntu 4, Ruby 2, and the twins 2 months. I thought it would be a good idea for me to stay there, look after my sister's minor children and my 14 year old baby sister. It would give me time to gain my strength and energy back and see what the future looked like for my mother. Once again, I was made to feel unwelcome at my mother's home. There were family members who were concerned about who was going to take care of us, how long I was going to stay with all those kids. Tasso did not have a "job", etc. etc. (They considered his business unacceptable and accused him of selling drugs). It would take too much time to tell you about all the ways in which I was reminded that I was not wanted there! There was just so much I could take!

Tasso had returned to Auburn to continue to work, take care of our place there, and make arrangements for us to go back to the city as soon as things got settled with my mother. He would come to Ashland every week to see us, bring me money, and make sure we were okay. After we had been there for a few months and he came for what he thought was a visit, I had my bags packed and was ready to return to Auburn with him. The way things were going, I knew if I stayed it would only be a matter of time before me or someone else got hurt. I had to leave! I could not continue to stay someplace when it was so obvious my presence was not wanted or appreciated. I could not continue to subject my children to all of the subtle, yet obvious, mistreatment and lack of love and respect I was feeling! Once again, I left Ashland with only a few clothes in a lawn sized trash bag in a borrowed car! Only this time, I had four children with me!

Tasso was really caught off guard as he had not quite finished making arrangements for us to return to Atlanta. We ended up in Tuskegee at the building where his friend manufactured furniture. It was really a large open building with no walls, no plumbing, no bathroom, or kitchen. We put up large sheets of heavy duty plastic to make a "bedroom" for us. We had two mattresses on the floor (ground), and a large table where we had our meals. Furniture was made on one side, we lived on the other.

[103]

There was no electricity on our side, so we used candles at night. We spent our days outdoors. Tasso would bring us two huge containers filled with water every morning and we had our section outside that was our "bathroom". We ate lots of canned salmon, salad, lots of fruit, baked beans, and sandwiches. The kids were having fun! It was like a great big adventure for them! They thought we were on a camping trip as we would go walking through the woods all day, collecting leaves, bugs, and doing whatever I could think of to keep them entertained. They woke up happy and excited about our "adventures" every day and went to bed at night with full bellies and lots of hugs and kisses from Mom and Dad. They had no idea that Mom and Dad were functioning in stress mode!

I think back now and realize that our children could have been taken away from us if anybody had known that we were living under such conditions. I thank God that nobody even cared enough about us to be concerned! Tasso and I never gave up on the plans we had for ourselves and our family! He always had a dream and a vision and I always supported him! He always had a plan and he worked hard every day to achieve his goals. All we had was each other and our children. We never gave up! We recovered and survived! God is Always Good!

Chapter Seventeen

After what I now call, the "nightmare years", I knew a change had to be made and I felt like if we didn't make a move soon, we would be stuck in the nightmare forever! I did not know anything except that we were too intelligent and had too many hopes and dreams for ourselves and our children to be stuck in a "nowhere" life! We had to make a change!

After my mother's accident, while the kids and I were staying in Ashland, we put all of our furniture and physical possessions in storage at the "shop", while we could finalize plans for our move back to Atlanta. Somehow, everything we owned was "stolen", and once again we were robbed of all of our physical possessions. One day, when I knew I couldn't take it anymore, I put everything we owned in a big green lawn-sized trash bag, we borrowed a truck, and headed back to Atlanta! I did not know where we would stay or what we would do; I just knew we had to make a move! It felt like it was now or never!

When we got to Atlanta, I called my flight attendant friend who had bought a house in East Point. I told her we were coming to town for the weekend to visit! We had always kept in touch and she was happy that we were coming to visit. Lucky for us, she happened to be in town at the time! The kids and I stayed at her place and Tasso went off to work his magic and make something happen for us! He told me he would be back on Sunday! I trusted him and believed that over the weekend he would pull something together for us! On Sunday, it got to be late afternoon and

Tasso had not showed up! On the outside, I may have looked calm, but on the inside, I was frantic! What would we do if he didn't show up!? My friend would have let us stay with her, but she was a single woman still working as a flight attendant. I would not have dared moved in on her with four kids! But, let me tell you how God worked in my life!

That evening, just as I was about to go into panic mode and break down and explain my real situation to my friend, my other flight attendant friend came by to visit. She too was so distraught over her life situation. She was married, a mother to three, and was still flying. It was hard as her husband was self-employed, trying to build his glass manufacturing and installation business, and they were trying to raise a family and maintain their home. She was in need of help as it was hard to find someone trustworthy that she could leave in their home with her husband and her children while she was off on two and three day trips. She said, "Cynthia, I really wish you could stay and help me out"! I could not believe my ears! I told her, "it just so happens I can stay". Neither of them knew how desperate my situation was! It was the answer to my prayers! We packed up our belongings and moved across town to stay with my friend and her family. God had worked out a solution to both of our problems!

My friend and her husband had a beautiful home in Lithonia, Ga. in an area of town that was strictly upper middle class. She had to leave on a three-day trip the next morning, so I was left there with my four kids, her three kids, and a house that looked like it had not been properly cared for in a while. To show my appreciation for her kindness, I went to work! I cleaned that house from top to bottom. The basement downstairs was covered with dirty laundry. My friend admitted she would often times go buy the children a week's worth of new clothes as that was easier than doing laundry! I cranked up that washer and dryer in the basement and when she got home from her trip, the house was clean, laundry had been done, dinner was ready, and she had a bubble bath and glass of wine waiting for her! Needless to say, she was extremely happy!

Our children were all close together in age. My oldest son enrolled in kindergarten with her oldest son. Kindergarten was half days back then; her son went to the morning session, my son went to the afternoon session. The other kids were home with me. I was shown how to get food stamps, so we had plenty of food and I was always in the kitchen making something to eat. Her husband was happy that I was there as he was enjoying coming home to a home-cooked meal every day. He was sort of a skinny guy and he even started putting on some weight! My friend had a live-in babysitter and housekeeper she could trust. The situation was mutually advantageous for both of us!

Our husbands even started doing business together. Her husband was a master in creating beveled glass walls and furniture (a style design that was popular in the 80's) and when Tasso saw what he could do, he went to work! As I said before, he was quite a salesman, and the next thing you knew, the business was growing by leaps and bounds! Tasso secured contracts and orders for glass installation with businesses, as well orders for custom designed furniture pieces for individual homeowners.

Tasso was extremely busy as he was living between Atlanta and Auburn. He had enrolled in graduate school at Auburn University and he was attending classes and waiting for the student loan money to process. At that time, student loans and schools worked differently than they do now. It was easier to get larger sums of money over and beyond what you may have needed for school to use as you needed! That money along with the money he helped generate through the glass business helped us be able to afford our own place again! We were even able to get a car and once again, we were on our way!

It was right around this time, that I became pregnant again! Yes, another method of birth control that failed. I kid you not! Our children were 6, 4, 2, and 2, and we did not plan on another. We told our friends we were expecting another baby and at the same time told them that we would be moving into our own place. My friend's husband did not want us to leave! He talked about how he could convert their basement into a living space for us, but we did not want them to alter their home and take on that additional expense just for us. As it turned out, my friend never told her husband that we were going to be staying there in the first place! He and I just happened to be talking one night, and he said that at first, he kept wondering when we were going to leave, but that since I was cooking, cleaning, and taking care of the kids, he just decided not to say anything. I was shocked to learn that my friend never discussed our being there with him! But, it was so like her!

[108]

At any rate, after several months of living with them, we got an apartment in Stone Mountain and moved out on our own. I will always be grateful to both of them for their kindness, hospitality, generosity, love, and support! They were instrumental in helping us get a fresh start in the city again!

Chapter Eighteen

I would like to say that the worst of our struggles were over, but that's far from it! The business relationship between my friend's husband and mine deteriorated. There was a third business partner who became jealous of the business relationship between the two of them. Instead of realizing they all had special talents that could be utilized to help the business grow for everyone, he began to undermine a lot of the business dealings. Tasso found it difficult to operate when he had to worry about somebody doing everything they could to make sure things did not go well. Once we moved out, that business relationship ended.

Tasso accepted a job in a management training program with Church's Chicken. He worked long hours and brought home lots of chicken, but the job did not pay the salary that was promised and once again, we found ourselves unable to keep up with the bills. It was during this time that Tasso brought his homeboy and close friend from the military up from Alabama to stay with us. He was looking for a new beginning, was unemployed, and was unable to contribute any financial assistance. It was quite stressful to have another adult in the house that could not help Tasso out. After a few months, he found work as a personal trainer at the YMCA and moved into their facility downtown. By this time, we had fallen behind on the rent again and were forced to move out. We also lost our car.

We left the apartment in Stone Mountain and stayed in an apartment with a friend of Tasso's niece in Decatur. We were staying there when I gave birth to our youngest son. Ishaaq was born July 5, 1985, and even in spite of our dire circumstances, Tasso was once again elated to have another son! Tasso was still in search of a business opportunity where he could be his own boss, but had yet to find something that would be profitable. When Ishaaq was born, he took the other children to stay with his sister in Alabama for a week. Ishaaq and I stayed in a local motel while Tasso worked to secure us another place to live.

He found an apartment he thought we could afford back in South Fulton County not too far from Harriet Tubman Elementary School. That was great because our oldest son, Ashuntu was ready for kindergarten and we could walk him to school every day. Regardless of what was going on with us, we always made sure that our son never missed a day of school. Tasso found a job with the Veterans Administration downtown and we finally thought we had caught a break!

However, after he brought home his first paycheck of $250.00 (net), he knew he would never be able to take care of us on that salary. Rent was $350.00 and he knew that with a wife and now five children to support, that was not going to work. His brother came from Alabama to live with us and had a job, but made no effort to contribute to the living expenses. Things really came to a crossroads, when one day as Tasso was leaving for work, Jamaal accidentally closed the front door on Jamilah's hand and her fingernail was practically removed from her hand. They were

[112]

about two years old at the time. We did not have a car and he was carpooling with a co-worker who was kind enough to transport them to the hospital. When Tasso called them at work to tell them about the emergency, they told him he did not have any sick leave and he would have to immediately report to work or he would be fired. Needless to say, that was the end of that job! He was not about to leave his child at home in pain and suffering just for a job! Once again, we got behind on the rent and were being evicted from our apartment.

God has always been at work in our lives, even when we may not have realized it! It just so happened that I had enrolled in graduate school at Mercer University and the same day we were being evicted, the school called and told me my student loan check for $5,000.00 was available for pickup. Tasso's co-worker drove us to Macon where I picked up the check.

We stayed in a motel for a couple of days until we were able to secure another apartment on Camp Creek Parkway. His brother knew we would have to move, but he never offered any type of help in any way! He just packed his bags and left! That is the reason Tasso never allowed him to live in our home again. His brother had proven that he didn't really care anything about us by the fact that he just walked out and never even asked if we had any place to go or if we needed any help. Actions always speak louder than words and we heard him loud and clear! Tasso never stopped doing whatever he could to help him or any of his siblings, for that matter, they just could not live with us anymore!

[113]

When we moved to the apartment on Camp Creek, Tasso took a job with a local taxicab company. He would pick up a car every morning. He had to make enough to pay $40.00 a day to pay for the car and the rest of the money was his. That worked out for a while, but it was very difficult. He had to do a lot of driving to make a good day's pay and with his back injury, driving all day was hard. I tried to help out! We had a neighbor who was a single mother with two children; one was in school, the other about 4 years old. I agreed to watch her younger daughter for her and pick up the older child from school. The school was in walking distance and both our children were attending there. This arrangement gave me a few dollars a week. It was not really enough to make a dent in the budget, but every little bit helped. Things improved for us, but then... Tasso had gotten a speeding ticket in the city and when he could not pay the fine, his driver's license was suspended! Since driving the taxi was the main source of income, he could no longer pay the rent and once again we lost our apartment!

I would like to say that no one helped us out during these rough days, but that would be far from the truth. I did have an aunt that I called during one of our critical moments when all resources had been exhausted and we were desperate for cash. One year, I had filed income taxes and was expecting a sizable income tax refund. However, instead of the check, I got a letter saying my refund had been held to pay back student loans. It was odd because at the time, I had been paying the agreed upon amount of $50.00 per month. Once the refund was held, there was nothing I could do! I told Tasso that I would ask my aunt for help. He did not want me to and asked me not to, but I went against his wishes and asked my aunt for the money anyway. I had to put the best interest of my children before any pride.

I will never forget that day! I stood in the pay phone booth, with tears in my eyes and asked her for $200.00. She agreed to give it to me, but not without some very harsh and hurtful words. I was "living with that man in sin who had no job and wouldn't marry me, I had all those kids, I needed to have myself checked out as I must be mentally ill, etc." Oh, I got quite the earful! I stood there, not saying a word. All that mattered at the moment was that she was going to send me the money. I promised to pay the money back and have been in a position to do so many times, but the way she made me feel that day, I figured I earned it for listening to all of the negative, degrading insults and untruths I had to listen to on that day. I don't know why I was surprised. It's pretty much the way she made me feel my whole life about anything I did.

There was another time, when I believe God sent an angel to help us. We were staying in a Motel 6 and Tasso had gone to pick up a taxi to make enough money to pay for the room and food for another day. However, it was a slow day and by noon he had not returned. He had not been able to make enough money to pay for the room. We had no choice but to vacate. I was standing on the corner like I was waiting for the bus. I had no money, five babies, and nowhere to go. I figured if it got dark and he did not return, I would find my way to a homeless shelter.

[115]

As I was standing there, a heavyset, white man pulled up in one of those old school long Cadillacs. There was a young black teenaged boy and girl in the car with him. He asked if he could help me. I said, "No, thank you, I am waiting for my husband". He said, "It's hot outside. Let me pay for you and the babies a room until he comes back". I thought it odd that he had such young kids in the car with him and I suspected something might be funny with that situation. Once again, I said, "No, thanks!" He stated that he was staying at the motel, would be glad to pay for us a room for the night, and my husband could pay him back when he returned. I was desperate, it was hot, and the babies were restless, so I finally agreed. However, I did make it clear, that my husband was going to return and that neither I nor my children would be involved in doing anything to repay his kindness. He laughed, sent the young black guy in to pay for us a room, gave us the key, and left.

When Tasso returned, I told him about the man. He went to his room, they talked, and he loaned Tasso enough money to pay for our room for the rest of the week. At the end of the week, when Tasso had made enough money to pay the man back, he was gone. No one at the front desk or any of the cleaning staff remembered him by name or by sight (he weighed all of 500 pounds, you would have remembered him if you had seen him)! It was as if he just vanished into thin air! This was another time that God made me realize his power and his presence in my life!

By this time, school was out. It was summer and we were basically homeless again. Tasso made friends with an East Indian guy who owned a motel on Old National Hwy and he let us stay in the same room every day for a while. The kids and I spent most of our days in the park, playing ball and having picnics. Our daughter drew a picture of us in the park playing ball. I still have that picture. They were having fun, but Dad and I were in stress mode trying to figure out a solution to our problem! Tasso had a friend who knew the owner of some apartments in East Point and he agreed to let us rent one of the empty apartments. Tasso continued driving the taxis and by the time school started back, I found a job at a hotel on Virginia Avenue and things were beginning to look better for us.

I worked the night shift from 11pm to 7am. No one else wanted the night shift. The manager knew I had small children and it worked out great! Tasso would pick up the cab about 6am, pick me up from the hotel and drive Ashuntu and Ruby, to school. I would be home with the twins and Ishaaq while he worked all day. He would pick the kids up from school around 3, do a little more driving, take the cab back, and be home by 7pm. I would make dinner, make sure homework was done, put the kids to bed by 8pm, maybe get an hour nap, and head to the hotel. It was just down the street from where we lived, so I walked most of the time. It was hard, but we were working it out. Through it all, we still managed to maintain a healthy relationship and we were still very much in love. It seemed that with each crisis, we drew closer to each other and became more determined to be successful! Once again, it changed!

It was already dangerous for me to be walking alone, but one night I was running late. It was starting to rain, and I accepted a ride from a man at the gas station who had offered. He looked harmless enough. However, when I got in the car, and he hit the automatic locks, it occurred to me what a risk I had taken. I was thinking, what if he drives past this hotel or goes in the opposite direction. No one will probably ever know what happened to me until they find my body someplace! Fortunately, the gentleman was honest and took me straight to work. I breathed a sigh of relief and thanked him, but I never did that again! It was a really long time before I told Tasso what I had done. If I had, that would have been the end of that job for sure!

If that wasn't enough, the manager who hired me now decided she wanted to give the night shift to her friend. She told me one Friday morning, that on Monday, I would have to work from 7am to 3pm. I explained to her that it would be impossible for me to work those hours as I was not making enough money to put three children in daycare. I was told no show, no job! So you know what happened…that was the end of that job! We seriously could not seem to catch a break!

While I was grateful for the apartment, it really was a dump! It was dark, dingy, and the kitchen was horrible! I really hated that space! We eventually put together enough money to move to a better, larger apartment on Roosevelt Highway and things started to get better for us. By this time, the twins had started school and only Ishaaq was at home. I had decided to go back to work and started to substitute teach in the Fulton County School system. Tasso's friend and his girlfriend had split up and the girlfriend and had moved into the same apartment complex we were now living in on Roosevelt Hwy. She was sharing her apartment with her two daughters and the oldest daughter agreed to babysit Ishaaq whenever I accepted a school assignment. That was great, as we knew this was someone we could trust. Most of the time, I worked at the elementary school the kids were attending so not only was I able to earn some money, I was able to go to school with them and monitor what was going on in their world. I eventually found another job as a ticket agent with a company called AMR, a subsidiary of American Airlines. They handled flights for Air Jamaica and Sabena Airlines. They only had flights out of Atlanta on the weekends so I worked at the school on the weekdays and at the airport on the weekends. Once again, things were beginning to move in a positive direction.

Tasso had decided to start his own business. We formed T & M Enterprises (Thomas and Mitchell) and Tasso was looking for some projects. He got started in the construction business by trying to help out some of his homeboys. There were two brothers who were master dry wall installers. They were always complaining to Tasso about how they were working like slaves and not making any money. Tasso was out one day and passed by some houses being built in South Fulton County. The framing was up, but needed dry wall. He stopped by and asked the construction manager if they had dry wall installers yet. The gentleman told him "No, give me an estimate and I will look it over". Tasso got together with the brothers, took them to the job site and had them estimate the job for him. They gave Tasso their estimate. Tasso doubled the number they gave him, presented it to the contractor, and he was awarded the job! (He later learned that was called General Contracting.)

T & M Enterprises was off and running! He incorporated, obtained a general contractor's license, and began bidding for jobs on the city, county, and state level. One of the first contracts he got was with MARTA (Metro Atlanta Rapid Transit Authority) at the College Park Train Station. He was hired to do the landscaping, which is still in place today. While on that job, he met a retired MARTA engineer who recognized Tasso's intelligence, ability, and desire to learn the business. The engineer was looking for someone who could partner with him in his business and a new partnership was born!

Tasso credits the engineer for teaching him how to bid contracts, read blueprints, and how to estimate jobs! They worked on many a successful venture together! Things had really started to take shape for us. Business was good, money was coming in, and we were happy! Things were looking good for a change!

Chapter Nineteen

By this time, it was 1989...Tasso had been granted a 10% disability by the Veterans Administration (which amounted to $90 a month). He had started to work on his disability rating when Ashuntu was born in 1978. He was always suffering with back pain and he was constantly taking time to go to the VA Hospital in Tuskegee, leaving me at home alone to handle all the responsibilities of the kids by myself. As you can imagine, that created quite a bit of tension in our relationship. We were always very much in love with each other, but I always hated anytime away from him. However, Tasso was very determined to get the military to compensate him for his back injury. When he was on a mission, and he had a plan, pretty much nothing or no one could deter him from his goal. That was one of the things I admired about him; his strength in the face of adversity and his ability to remain true to his vision. I could fuss, I could argue, but he knew what he had to do. He told me that one day it would all pay off. I always believed in him. He had never let me down when it really counted. I shared in his vision and I knew what he was telling me was right. It was just hard!

We still had not legally married. Tasso had received a divorce decree from his first "marriage". His "wife" asked for no spousal or child support. Tasso took that as a sign that he must not have been the father. At any rate, we were going through so much, there wasn't much thought given to the subject of us getting legally married. We had been joined together in our hearts, bodies, souls, and spirit, since May 31, 1976, and not much consideration was given to a legal union. However, our children were getting older and we were not getting any younger. Tasso wanted to make sure we would have access to all of the benefits he was working so diligently to receive from the VA. We decided to go ahead and tie the knot!

We both agreed that we should actually marry on May 31st since that was the day when we had already been brought together by a higher power. When May 31st came around in 1989, we were both short on cash and it was looking like we would have to wait another year! Yet, once again, God was at work! Around noon, just as we had come to terms with the fact that we would plan for the next year, the mailman came and in the mail, there was a check! Since the kids were at school, we were able to leave Ishaaq with the neighbor and take the bus to the courthouse where we were able to wed in a civil ceremony! We made it back home just in time to get the kids off the bus, do homework, have dinner, and put the kids to bed. It was back to business as usual for us, except now we were legally, Mr. and Mrs. Tasso and Cynthia Thomas!!!!

Chapter Twenty

Once we had legally married, we became serious about finding a home for us to raise our family in. Business with T & M had been good and we had more than ten thousand dollars saved up in a shoebox under the bed. (Tasso did not trust banks with all his money). Tasso told me to find the house and he would take care of the rest. It took almost two years of looking for me to find a house that I thought would fit our needs. When I finally found a house, Tasso did all the paperwork and I showed up at the closing. I signed all the necessary paperwork and three days before my 39th birthday, we received the keys to our new home. Tasso tossed me the keys and said, "Happy Birthday, baby!" We were so excited!

I never brought the kids to the house until moving day. When we unlocked the door and let them in, it was as if they automatically knew where to go. Ruby and Jamilah ran down the hallway to the master bedroom upstairs, Ashuntu had the smallest bedroom across the hallway all to himself, Jamaal and Ishaaq shared the larger bedroom next to his, and Tasso and I had the downstairs bedroom, den with the fireplace, and office all for us.

Years earlier, I was bored one day and was dreaming of the house that I wanted us to have. I wrote it all down on a sheet of paper… four bedrooms, downstairs suite for us, office for Tasso, garage, patio, backyard for the kids to play in, and a large kitchen. One day, as I was going through some old paperwork, I ran across that sheet of paper. I had actually described the house that we were currently living in! It was many years later when I learned about how the power of writing things down would actually help bring them into existence. It actually does work! It was another time in my life when God made his presence in my life visible to me!

Many of the things Tasso had planned for and dreamed of began to take shape as well. He started a new corporation, Ossat Construction, had a team of dedicated workers, continued work as a general contractor specializing in concrete flatwork, and scored several big contracts over the next few years with Clayton County, Dekalb County, and with Clark Atlanta University, to name a few. I had taken a full time job with the State of Georgia as a caseworker the year before we moved into the house and had a steady income with insurance benefits and paid time off. No more being homeless for us! Tasso had a new truck. I had a new car. The kids were doing very well in school and were involved in everything from band, orchestra, football, basketball, track, academic clubs, etc. We were very much a busy, healthy, and happy crew!

Tasso always maintained a relationship with his siblings. They were very important to him. He always kept in touch with them and he loved them all very much. Even though they were barely cordial to me, I was used to it. I wanted them to love me because Tasso loved me. I wanted to love them because Tasso loved them. However, it got to a point where it didn't matter anymore. Tasso's love and devotion to me and our children was the only thing that mattered to me. They eventually began to see that nothing was going to tear us apart, and they slowly began to accept me and the children as their family.

Tasso always encouraged me to keep in touch with my family. He always encouraged me to connect with my siblings and would often ask me if I had called them. He never wanted to be the reason we lost touch. Even though my mother had been so unkind to him, he never uttered one single word against her, ever! He was, however, quite irritated with the people in my life who had caused me to have such low self-esteem, but he never spoke ill of any of them. Through his love, I was able to gain self-confidence and love for myself. I had always said, that no matter what ever happened between us, I would always love him because he gave me the ultimate gift, self-love! Without his love, I may have gone through my entire life hating and doubting myself. For that gift, I will always be grateful to him and to God for placing him into my life!

Tasso and I both were very family-oriented and most of our activities centered around our children. Nothing and no one else was more important to us! The happiness and well-being of the seven of us came first! We would have parties on Friday nights to celebrate the successful completion of another week. We would pick up pizza, movies, and ice cream. We'd come home and have fun! Birthdays were big too, as we would always celebrate with going out to dinner, with gifts and cake and ice cream back at home. There were visits to Six Flags over Georgia every summer and trips to the Zoo. We managed to take a couple of family vacations to San Francisco to visit my brother, to visit the beaches in

Savannah, Georgia, and Myrtle Beach in South Carolina. We even managed a trip to Jamaica! We tried to give our children as many different experiences as we could!

Tasso and I always managed to carve out some "us" time as well. We would have our little parties downstairs in our private suite after the kids had gone to bed. I would light some candles, Tasso would make a fire in the fireplace, have some wine for me, (Tasso was never much of a drinker), turn on some Isley Brothers, and it was on! Those parties make up some of my fondest memories!

Whenever Tasso did take me out, he knew how to wine and dine a lady! Once, after he and his business partner closed a particularly big deal, he gave me money for a fancy outfit and the gentlemen took their wives out on the town. We got my cousin to babysit, and we spent the night out at one of Atlanta's finest restaurants and jazz clubs. No expense was spared and it was a great night!

As the children got older, we even managed to take of couple of trips - just the two of us! We would sometimes get a hotel room in downtown Atlanta and pretend we were away for the weekend or sometimes we would drive to Florida and spend a couple of days. Tasso knew that I loved the beach and even though he was not fond of the water, he always let me plan a beach trip because he knew it would make me happy!

Our children continued to grow and one by one started to finish high school and head off to college. I could not believe it was all going by so fast! The first high school graduation was Ashuntu in 1997, he went off to Savannah State for a year, then came back home to attend Clark-Atlanta University. He eventually got his Bachelor's degree in Business Administration from the University of North Alabama in Florence, Alabama, in 2009.

Ruby graduated high school in 2000, went off to Xavier University in New Orleans and received her degree in Biology/Pre-Med in 2004. She returned to Atlanta to obtain a medical degree from the Morehouse School of Medicine in 2008, completed her pediatric residency in 2009, and went on to get a Master's degree in Public Health from the Morehouse School of Medicine in 2011. Ruby is a board certified pediatrician today and is on the faculty of the Morehouse School of Medicine. She married in 2013. Her father walked her down the aisle on her wedding day and she is now the mother of two boys.

The twins graduated high school in 2001 and went off to Auburn University. Jamilah graduated first in 2005 with a degree from the School of Education in Sports Medicine. She went on to obtain a Master's degree in Education from Alabama State University in 2008, and received her Specialist's degree in Education from Mercer University in 2016. Jamilah teaches middle school, has coached her middle school girls basketball team to the Final Four, is married, and the mother of a daughter.

Jamaal received his degree in Aerospace Engineering from Auburn in 2006. He remained in Auburn after graduation and obtained a job at an aerospace engineering facility. He married his college sweetheart and was the first to make us grandparents, as he welcomed his first son into the world in 2010. They are now parents to a daughter and another son who is named after Tasso.

Our youngest, Ishaaq graduated from high school in 2005 and remained home to obtain his Associate's Degree in Computer Networking and Security Systems from the Hi-Tech Institute. He lives at home with me and is my personal assistant, chauffeur, chef, and my computer tech guy!

Through it all, we have remained a close-knit family, celebrating and enjoying each moment. All the hard times and the sacrifices were worth everything we had been through! Tasso and I had always stressed the importance of education. We knew it was the only way to ensure some type of success in this world. We expected and accepted nothing less than the best of each one of our children. They followed our rules, did everything we asked of them, and they made it a joy to be parents. They continue to be a constant source of pride and joy!

Chapter Twenty-One

Tasso and I still managed to remain in love with each other. Our relationship was not without its challenges over the years. It was extremely difficult at times! The majority of our challenges stemmed from financial difficulties. He was self-employed and the stresses of owning and operating his own business were difficult. He was met with obstacles at every turn. Being a minority general contractor had its own set of challenges, but, he managed to remain true to himself and operate a successful construction business. He was very well respected by his employees and all those who came in contact with him in his various business dealings. He was always fair and treated his employees well. There were times when he was shorted on his pay for various reasons (he was a black general contractor, need I say more), but he always paid his employees whatever they were due even if that meant he came home with $500.00 instead of $5,000.

My job with DFACS was also quite stressful! I always seemed to be one of those people who worked hard, worked well, but was always faced with some type of drama at every turn. I can see now that it was God's way of telling me I didn't belong there. I was too busy with my own agenda to pay attention! I withstood it for 15 years. In December of 2006, I finally decided to quit! I was seven years short of my retirement date, but I could no longer tolerate the levels of abuse and disrespect that I had been subject to since day one. Tasso had been telling me to quit for several years, as he was tired of seeing me come home so defeated and frustrated. But, I did not want to place the entire financial burden on him again. He always assured me he could handle it and it would never be like it was in the days past! Once again, he was right! When I left, it seemed as though I had access to more money than I did when I was working! The only thing I regretted was that I hadn't done it sooner! Leaving was one of the best decisions I ever made!

I did, however, suffer something of an emotional breakdown. It was like I had been moving at the speed of light and all of a sudden everything came to a dead stop! I had no job, the children were on their own, and I did not remember who I was or what I really wanted to do with my life for myself. It was like all of the things that had been bothering me all of my life presented themselves to me at once and I was overwhelmed! I couldn't handle it! Being a wife and mother was great, but who was I really? What did I really want to do with my life!?

From 2007 through 2010, I spent many days depressed, sad, and unable to sleep or eat. I was prescribed anti-depressants, but never took them. I have never been much of a pill-taker and I knew the answer to my problems was not in a pill bottle. I was trying everything I could not to be depressed! I had more of my identity wrapped up in my "job" than I ever thought I did, and when I didn't have it any more I felt worthless. I know that's really sad, but that's how I felt. I even briefly contemplated taking my own life. I felt so bad one day that I sat in the car, in the garage with the engine running, windows up, just wanting the bad feeling to stop. In

[130]

the flash of a moment, I knew that my youngest son would be looking for me and would find me slumped over in the car! I could not let him have that image of me in his head for the rest of his life! I turned off the car, let the windows down, and knew that I would have to find another way to feel better as killing myself was not the answer! I thank God that He allowed me to have that moment of clarity!

Tasso had tried everything he could think of to make me happy, but it was not him, it was me! One day, he took me to the emergency room at a local hospital because he didn't know what else to do. A nurse pulled me to the side and told me if I didn't get my act together, they were going to drug me, classify me as a threat to myself and others, and lock me up in the psychiatric ward! That did not sound like it anything I wanted to do! She advised me to see a doctor and try anti-depressants (I had been there, had done that), or I could go see a mental health counselor.

Well, now, I had always been one to think that sitting down talking to some stranger about my problems could not possibly help. After all, I believed in God and talked to Him all the time. What good could come of me talking to some stranger about my problems?! I had tried everything else and nothing worked so as a last resort, I decided to go. It was one of the best decisions I had ever made! It saved my life! Part of my therapy was to become more physically active. I joined a local gym and discovered Zumba and yoga! Those two forms of exercise helped me on my road to recovery. They are still an important part of my life today.

At the time I sought help at a mental health facility, my health benefits had lapsed. I maintained my own health insurance when I was employed and once I resigned, they ended. It took a minute for the VA to add me on under Tasso's plan. In the meantime, I had to a go to a mental health clinic where they would treat people without insurance. The intake worker I saw told me she would assign me to a therapist called "J".

After a few months of seeing "J", I was able to return to my old self. I felt stronger and better! She helped me resolve my feelings and reclaim my life! When my insurance benefits were restored, I was so grateful for all the help I had received from the counseling center and from my personal therapist that I wanted to go back as a paying customer. I wanted to pay for the services that helped get me back to myself! I called the center one day and asked to speak to her and nobody seemed to know who she was. I went there in person and the staff looked at me like they had no clue who I could have been talking about! It was like she was there for me, and now she was gone! This was another time when God placed a special angel of his in my life. I know of no other way to explain it! I vowed right then and there to try and live my life in a way that God would be proud that he created me!

I decided to return to school in 2010 to pursue a Master's degree in Mental Health Counseling. I thought if I could help one person the way that going to counseling had helped me, it would be a truly great thing! For the first time in my life, I felt like I knew what I wanted my life's work to be outside of being a wife and mother.

I enrolled in online classes in a three year counseling studies program at Capella University. It was the beginning of a whole new life for me! Along with enjoying being a wife and mother, I was enjoying school, being a grandmother, meeting new people, having new experiences. Life was good!

Tasso was beginning to decrease his workload and was semi-retired. He was spending more time at home. A few years earlier, he had finally gotten his 100% disability rating from the VA for his back injury and the other conditions that arose as a result of being in chronic pain over the years. He had been working on this for over 20 years. He finally had his monthly check, which was enough to maintain our home, and we did not have to stress over money the way we had in the past. He was enjoying spending time with the grandkids and was becoming a man of leisure! We were settling into being an "old, married couple" and being grandparents. Life was great!

Sometimes when things start to go too well, it makes you wonder what is coming up next. We were about to find out!

Part Five

We ended….

November 5, 2013

Chapter Twenty-Two

November 3, 2013

Life was happening as usual. Tasso had just returned from a trip to the Veteran's Hospital in Tuskegee, Alabama. The VA in Tuskegee had been his main source of treatment and support from day one. After a few days, he was still not feeling well and decided to go the VA Hospital in Decatur. He returned with a diagnosis of a strained muscle, a prescription for some 800 mg Ibuprofen, and rest.

I was busy with school. My classes were 10 week classes and I was in week 5 of my final class. Talk of graduation was in the air as I was at the end of my 3 year program. Ruby had gone to a medical conference in Boston, her husband had gone with her, and they left Kwame with us for the weekend. Kwame loved being with us! Pop, as Tasso was called, was his best buddy! I was coming down with a cold and did not feel well myself. In the midst of all of this, I remember Tasso calling me downstairs where he was sitting on the couch. He grabbed my arm and told me, "When I tell you I am in pain, you really need to pay attention to me". Often times I would try and distract his attention away from his pain by telling him to focus more on the positive things rather than the negative, but I promised him that I would be more attentive.

Earlier that day, I had called a tree cutter to come over. I wanted to have him trim down some of the trees (they were supposed to be hedges) that were growing out of control and were all over the side of the house. The tree man had done the job, but had left all of the branches in a gigantic pile on the side of the house which is not what we had discussed! I now had all of these tree branches up against the house. I wanted to move them because I didn't want unwanted pests to find a new home under them and create further problems.

Earlier that morning, I had opened the front door to go outside and there was this bird sitting on the railing of the front porch. It looked like a pigeon, but had a wider backside, more like a duck. I thought it was an unusual looking bird! We have lived in our subdivision for more than 20 years and I had *never* seen a pigeon in the area. I don't like birds and have had a "bird phobia" for as long as I can remember, so I didn't want to go anywhere near it! I immediately slammed the door, thinking it would fly away, but it didn't! I opened and closed the front door one more time, but the thing didn't budge! I called Tasso and told him about the bird. Knowing about my bird phobia, he got up, went outside, stayed a minute or two, and came back in. He told me, "he let me pet him". What the heck?! I thought that was odd. Tasso was not afraid of birds or any other animals that I knew of for that matter, however, I thought it was unusual for him to actually touch it. I was so freaked out! I told him, "don't you touch me or anything in this house until you go wash your hands!" I was so busy with everything else that was going on, I didn't give it anymore thought. I did, however, look out of the window to see if the bird was gone. It was not on the porch anymore, but, it was waddling back and forth in front of the garage doors. Ishaaq pulled up in the car a few minutes later and saw it. He thought it would fly away when he pulled up, but it didn't! It waddled back and forth for a few more minutes. By the time Ishaaq came inside and I looked back out, it was gone! Finally!

Later that afternoon, Tasso told me he still wasn't feeling well and wanted Ishaaq to drive him over to the local hospital. I didn't want him to go and I didn't think he needed to, but I had learned over the years that when he was determined to do something, it was pretty much useless to try and change his mind. I did not have the energy for an argument, so I told him to go ahead and I would see him when he got back. Imagine my surprise when Ishaaq called me from the hospital a few hours later and told me that Dad was being admitted and that he would be having surgery! What!? Ishaaq came home to stay with Kwame and I headed to the hospital.

Tasso did not want to go into surgery until I got there. I spoke with the nurse and she assured me that if I was on the way, they would honor his request and wait until I was there before taking him to surgery. Our daughter, Ruby, who is a physician, had already spoken with Tasso and the surgeon who happened to be a colleague of hers from the Morehouse School of Medicine. They had already discussed his treatment plan. It was a routine procedure which was usually done on an outpatient basis. No problem! Tasso thought his daughter was a medical expert on every subject so I was not surprised he had consulted with her first. That was

[139]

okay with me! As long as everything was okay with them, it was okay with me!

I ran into traffic leaving the house and had to take an alternate route so it took a little longer for me to get to the hospital than usual. They waited as long as they could, but by the time I finally arrived, Tasso was already in surgery. I was nervous and anxious, but I was only there about 30 minutes when the surgeon came out and talked to me. He told me everything went well. He wanted to keep Tasso overnight mainly because of his age and to give him a round of antibiotics intravenously. He expected a full recovery and discharge on the next day. Great news!

Tasso came out of surgery more alert and awake than I expected which I thought was a good sign. I stayed with him the rest of the day and night. I slept on the couch in his room. Even though he was alert, he was unusually quiet. I was glad to see him calm and resting.

Chapter Twenty-Three

November 4, 2013

I needed to go home to shower, change clothes, and check on Kwame who was being attended to by his Uncle Ishaaq. Ashuntu and Jamilah came to the hospital to sit with Tasso. While I was gone, the nurse was supposed to come in, give him a bath, and change his gown. By the time I got back later that afternoon, she had not done so. I was upset that he had spent all day without his bath and change of clothes. She then offered to do it, but I told her, "No, he is my husband. I will do it myself!" Ashuntu and Jamilah left. The nurse gathered the necessary supplies for me and I began to give Tasso his bath. He told me, I don't want to be cold". I assured him that I would keep him warm.

Tasso was a proud man and the last thing he ever wanted was to be helpless and unable to care for himself. However, he sat up on the side of the bed like a proud warrior and king and let me give him his bath. No words were spoken. I washed his face. I washed his upper body, arms, shoulder, and chest. I draped a towel around his shoulders. I was careful to keep each area covered as I washed him making sure he did not get cold. I changed him into a new gown and he settled in for a nap. He told me "Jamaal will be here soon". I did not know anyone had called Jamaal. It was minor surgery and I did not want to get him unnecessarily alarmed, so I had not had time or thought to call him. Tasso called him and told him he wanted to see him. Jamaal made his way to the hospital later that night. For some reason, the doctor did not make rounds that day and we knew we would be there for another night. No problem! It was one way I knew he would rest!

While Jamaal was there, Ishaaq came back to the hospital to visit with Tasso. Tasso was resting and Jamaal and Ishaaq were over in the corner, clowning around and being silly like they did when they were little boys. Tasso cleared his throat, and said, "Hey!" They cut it out! I thought it was so cute!

Later that evening, Ruby and her husband returned from Boston, and they came by with Kwame to visit with Tasso. Jamilah came by with a happy face balloon and a fruit vase from Edible Arrangements. She told Tasso all about her girls' basketball team (she was the head coach) and she talked about her latest plays and the all happenings with her team. We all noticed that Tasso was still quieter than anyone of us had ever known him to be, but we just thought he was resting. Tasso could not eat the fruit, the children were glad to help out with that, but the balloon and vase stayed on his bedside table to cheer him up! Even though he did not speak, we could tell he was present and enjoying the moment!

Later that evening, when everyone had gone home and it was time for bed, I asked Tasso, "Do you want me to sleep with you?" He said, "Yes". I tucked him in, took off my shoes and jacket, grabbed a blanket, and climbed up on the bed to sleep next to him. He stretched out his arm, and I settled into my favorite spot with my head on his shoulder and my hand on his chest. I remembered thinking that I would probably be awake all night, but to my surprise, I slept. I felt surprisingly rested when I woke up and I was excited. I knew we would go home today!

Chapter Twenty-Four

November 5, 2013

As we woke up, the sun was rising. We got up, used the bathroom, faced the East, and said our morning prayers together. Tasso got back into bed. I knew that before the doctors would discharge him, he would need to use the bathroom. I went to the cafeteria, got him a banana (he ate one every day), a green Naked Smoothie drink, and a bottle of water. I figured that would do the trick! I wanted everything to be in order so when the doctor made his rounds later that afternoon, we would be ready to go home. I had already begun to gather the necessary supplies from the hospital that would help me take care of him at home. I had instructed Ishaaq to put the TV in our bedroom because I knew it would be the best way to keep Tasso in bed once we got home. Tasso finished his snack, we took a walk around the hospital corridor (he didn't want to), and I got him back into bed so he could rest. I called the kids and told them Dad was sleeping. I informed them we had a good rest last night and were waiting for the doctor to come and discharge him later that day.

An hour or so later when I returned to the room, Tasso woke up and said "my chest hurts". I immediately pressed the call button, stepped to the door and saw that the nurse was on her way. I told him, "It's okay, the nurse is here". When the nurse came in, Tasso was having trouble breathing and she got him to take a couple of deep breaths with her. At the same time she said to the other nurse in the room that Mr. Thomas needs respiratory therapy. She called for additional help.

By this time, I started to see a white, foamy substance coming from the corner of Tasso's mouth, and I thought to myself, 'this can't be good', yet, I didn't feel panic. I was holding his hand, we were looking into each other's eyes, and I told him he would be okay. Suddenly, he had this look on his face, this look in his eye, like he was no longer looking at me, but looking through me. It was not a look of fear, just a look of slight surprise, like, "Oh..."

He let go of my hand and lay back as if he were asleep. I started to move my things out of the way so the medical team could come into the room to help him. I walked out into the hallway and when I turned around, I saw a male nurse administering CPR. The scene seemed to be floating backwards; like it was moving miles away from me. I remember thinking to myself, 'it will be okay, they do this all the time, he'll be fine'.

About that time, a nurse approached me and asked me if we had kids and if they lived in the city. I told her yes, all but one. She suggested that I call them. I had already called Ishaaq and Ashuntu earlier; they were on their way to the hospital. I could not reach Ruby, but called her husband and he assured me he would contact her. Jamilah was at school. At this point, I was beginning to get a little nervous. I told them Jamilah was a teacher and it may be hard to get her in the classroom, so I suggested they call her principal. I could no longer see what was happening in Tasso's room.

The next thing I noticed, there was a security guard and a chaplain standing nearby. The chaplain approached me and asked me if he could pray with me. I remember telling him, "I know how to pray. You want me to pray, I don't need you to help me pray. I can pray by myself." I walked into an empty room at the end of the hall, walked over to the window, which was facing east, and I just said, "Okay, God... Okay, God, you know what to do, God". I didn't know what to say or what I was supposed to say. I was still not aware of what was really happening. I figured enough time had passed and I needed to see what was going on with Tasso. The chaplain and security guard tried to prevent me from leaving the room. I was getting annoyed, and told them, "Do not touch me, I need to see what is going on. Please, move out of my way, and let me go and see about my husband". They did!

A nurse was walking along beside me and by the time I got halfway down the hall, she said, "Oh, good, here's the doctor, now. Let's go back in here (the empty room) so we can talk". I reluctantly agreed. The doctor wanted me to sit. I did not want to, but they would not talk until I did, so I sat. He began with, "we used all the available medicines and we were unable…"

That was all I heard. I told them, "oh no, I have seen enough TV medical shows to know that when you all come into the room with these speeches, something has happened, what did you do?" I left out of the room and returned to Tasso's room. He was lying there as if he was asleep. I climbed up on the hospital bed, straddled his body, and tried to make him put his arm around me. It kept falling off. I was patting his face and telling him, "I'm here, baby. You can wake up now, it's me. Baby, you can wake up now." I kept trying to put his arm around me, but it kept falling off, limp by the bedside. There was no response. His eyes were closed. Tasso had died! I remember asking, them, "What did you do to him? What did you do to him? He was fine. What did you do?"

By that time, I realized there were other people in the room. Ruby was sitting there with Kwame and her husband. I saw Ashuntu. I saw Ishaaq take one look at Dad and put his fist through the wall. I climbed down from the bed, took a look under the sheet, said a quick goodbye to that beautiful body, and walked away from the bedside. The surgeon came into the room making rounds as usual, and he was outraged! He said, "What the hell did you all do to my patient? What has happened here?" He was just as shocked as we were! There had been no complications from the minor surgery and he was coming to discharge Dad.

We all just stood around in the room, not knowing what to say or do. He asked the nurses and other medical personnel to step out of the room. We waited for Jamilah to come from school. She sat in a chair in the room, next to Tasso's bed, not letting anyone come near her Dad. We waited for Jamaal to arrive. When he got there, we all held hands around Dad's bed and said our prayer, Sura 1, from the Quran. Minutes passed and they seemed like hours. Hours passed and they seemed like minutes. There were questions: organ donation (NO), autopsy (YES), and moving Dad to the morgue (wait, what?).

I wanted to stay. We all did. I did not want to leave him there. How could I? How could I just walk away? The nurse assured me that we would not want to see them move him. It would be best for us to go home. I took her advice and we all decided to leave. We were all in shock! Oh, God. What just happened here and what do we do now? I did not know!

I remember riding in the car on the way home, feeling nothing but numbness. I called my sister. She said I whispered to her, "Tasso died", and hung up. I called Tasso's sister and said the same thing. I don't remember making either call. When I got home, I immediately took off the clothing I was wearing including the shoes. It was an outfit that Tasso had bought me. I put it in a trash bag and took it outside to the garbage can. I knew I would never want to see or wear that outfit again! I immediately had Ishaaq take the TV out of our bedroom. It would not be necessary since he would not be coming home. I got into the shower and I cried! I don't know how long I was in there! I just sat in the corner and I cried, I wailed, I moaned!

When I got out of the shower, the house was full of people. My sister and her boyfriend were there. My brother was on his way from Huntsville. He had made arrangements to have food and drink brought to the house. Tasso's brother (who lives in the city) and his wife were there. I must have been functioning on autopilot. I do remember thinking that the children were watching me and I had to be strong. I had to show them how to handle adversity, so I tried to present a calm front, but I was torn apart on the inside. It felt like someone had ripped my heart out of my chest and there was just a hole in its place. That feeling would last for quite some time. I don't know if I ate or slept. I just knew I had to keep putting one foot in front of the other. Ruby was pregnant and I knew she needed to rest, so I told her if she would lie down, I would too. Jamilah went straight to the back bedroom and closed the door. I don't remember too much else, it is all just a big blur!

The next few days were spent making arrangements for the autopsy and the funeral. We did not know what caused his death. We had to make sure his remains were handled respectfully. Tasso had been a Muslim since the early 70's and I knew he wanted an Islamic burial. We found a funeral home that would honor those requests. There is no embalming and no burial in a casket. The body is given a final washing by the sons or brothers from the mosque and shrouded in white cotton sheets. We opted to let the brothers from the mosque wash him, as we thought it might be too much for his sons.

Once I learned about the bathing ritual, I then understood why Tasso sat there so calmly and kingly as I bathed him in that hospital room. He knew that I, his Queen, was giving him his final bath. It was the final time I would get to be alone with him in such an intimate setting and provide such an intimate service for my King. I was honored and blessed to have had the privilege. We found an Imam (an Islamic minister) to conduct the service and we found a beautiful Islamic burial site. Arrangements had been made.

We buried Tasso on November 9, 2013. The ceremony was plain and simple as he would have wanted it. The boys, along with his best friend and spiritual brother recited the prayer, Sura I, from the Quran. Ruby honored her father with a few words. Jamilah asked to speak. I remember she thanked me for choosing her Dad as my partner. I spoke last, reading the words from an Anita Baker song that I had intended to be read at my funeral. Tasso's sons and brothers carried his body to his grave. His sons stood in his grave, received his body, and placed him on his side facing the East. We all wore white and were escorted to the funeral and burial site in white limousines. It was a beautiful service! We returned home to begin life without our husband, father, and King!

Chapter Twenty-Five

In the days immediately following Tasso's passing, I had some extraordinary experiences! Before his burial, I saw him. I was in the backyard, just outside getting some air, and I saw him. It was for a split second, in a blur, the way you have seen spirits portrayed in television and film. He was dressed in the same clothing he had on when he went to the hospital. He whizzed past me, smiling. I was in awe!

I had a picture of Tasso, the last one he had taken one day when he and his sons visited his sister. For some reason, I placed that picture right in front of me on the bathroom vanity where I could see it. The photograph seemed to be alive, the eyes seemed to be looking at me; watching me, until after we buried him. After that, it was just a photograph. It was as if the energy, life, and movement in the eyes were gone. I removed it from the vanity.

Tasso's spirit was in the house. The morning following his death, I was downstairs in the laundry room, ironing something to wear and I heard the door open with a loud creak. We never had creaking doors in the house, so I thought it was strange. I thought perhaps one of the boys was coming in from the garage, but no one was there. I returned to my ironing. A few seconds later, I heard a noise from our bedroom. There was a desk in the corner of our bedroom that I was planning to use as my desk for studying and reading. I had neatly placed two stacks of CD's on the desk for some project I was working on. The noise I heard was the CD's falling over onto the floor. It had to be Tasso. There was no other reason for them just to fall over. The same thing happened in the den downstairs. I had the rest of our CD's neatly stacked, in some sort of order that made sense to me. They, too, for some reason just toppled over. I knew he was there. He was letting me know even though he was gone, I was still not going to have everything neat and in order like I liked it!

I also had the experience of finding money. The day we went to buy the sheets to take to the funeral home for his burial and pay for the burial plot, I withdrew $200 from my bank account; two one hundred dollar bills. I gave one to Ruby to add to the money for the burial plot, and the other one I spent on the sheets for Tasso to be shrouded in. When I got back home, I still had a $100 bill in my purse. Over the next couple of days, I would open a book – there would be a $100 bill. I opened a drawer to put away some of Tasso's laundry – there was a $100 bill. I put my hand in his suit jacket pocket – there was a $100 bill. I knew it was Tasso. He was still taking care of me.

Tasso always made sure I had a $100 bill in my pocket. Any time I wanted to go shopping or out with my friends or family, he would always give me a $100 bill. I knew it was him! In the months that passed, as I was figuring out finances, I often asked him if he could still continue to drop me a bill or two from time to time! He has not!

The most amazing thing that happened, however, was yet to come. I kept the happy face balloon that Jamilah had brought to the hospital in our bedroom. The happy face was on one side; the other side was solid silver. No matter how I tried to keep the smiling happy face towards me, it kept turning back to the silver side. It was as if it was angry and did not want me to see the smiling, happy face. I decided that Tasso would not see the balloon anyway, so I might as well let it go. It would be like taking a step towards saying goodbye. I went out the backdoor into the backyard and let the balloon go. I thought it would go straight up into the air, but it didn't. It went up, around the corner and towards the front of the house. I followed it around the sidewalk and out into the front yard. The balloon floated towards the east, toward our neighbor's house two doors away, and landed in the top of their huge oak tree. I thought, great! Now everyone will know that I let the balloon go and every time we come out of the house we will have to see it.

I closed my eyes and said a silent prayer, "God please just let the balloon go ahead and float away". When I opened my eyes, it was gone! There was no wind that day; it was sunny and clear. I blinked a couple of times to make sure I was just not hallucinating and walked out into the middle of the cul-de-sac to make sure the balloon had not floated to the other side of the tree, it was really gone! I remember saying to myself, "Wow, God is really listening and he is hearing and answering my prayers right now". What an incredible feeling! What happened next is truly amazing!

I was standing there in the middle of the circle, ready to walk back towards my house, when I felt a warm breeze that began to swirl around my feet, in a circular motion. You could see the leaves begin to swirl. I was unable to move. I looked up and these two giant clouds that looked like arms and hands began to open up. Out of that opening, from the east, there was a single bird which looked to be an eagle. It flew out of the clouds, over my head. As I turned to watch it fly away, all of a sudden, it was gone, vanished into the air, just like the balloon. I immediately felt that it was a sign, that God was telling me that he had opened up his arms and let Tasso into his heavenly home. He had made it! I took great comfort in the fact that God let me know that Tasso had lived a good enough life to make it into His kingdom. I felt honored that God would give me a sign that would bring me such comfort. At that point, I decided that I would try and live my life well enough so that I, too, would be able to make it into God's kingdom and be reunited with my love.

Tasso came to me several times after he was buried. I was in bed one night and I was exhausted! It was of the first nights since he had died that I felt like I could actually sleep. I was sleeping on my side of the bed and I felt a nudge from behind me. You know the nudge one feels when you know your partner is ready for sex. I reached behind me and said, "No, not tonight baby. I need to sleep." I promise you, I felt something there. It was not pillows, it was not bed covers. It was his body that was there behind me. I did not turn to look, but as soon as I said no, he left. When I reached back to make sure what I had felt was real, it was no longer there. My arm fell flat against the mattress and it was only the bed that was there. As more time passed, and I really started to miss the sexual part of our relationship, I often wondered what would have happened if I had not said no that night.

He came to me one other time several months later. I had decided that I could no longer bear to continue to sleep in our bedroom. I decided to move upstairs into the master bedroom suite. It was the first time I had occupied the master suite in our home. The room had belonged to my girls when they were growing up at home. Since my youngest son, Ishaaq, was the only child still living at home, he had taken the room for himself. He understood my pain, and agreed to change rooms with me.

One night as I was getting out of the shower, I felt a force that caused me to drop to my knees! I was dripping wet from the shower, in nothing but a towel, and I was overcome with this feeling. It was if my entire body was caught up in some type of orgasmic spasmodic feeling, except it was a feeling that encompassed my entire body. I know of no other way to describe it or how intense the feeling was. I could do nothing but remain on my knees, with my head on the floor. I stretched out my arms in front of me (kind of like in a yoga - child's pose) and waited for the feeling to pass. After several minutes, the feeling went away and I was able to move. I stood up, dried off, and got dressed. I have not had that experience again. I can only think that it was Tasso coming to me once again.

I can also tell you that whenever someone dies, you should be very careful about the contact you make with them. When Tasso died, I touched his face. I wanted him to know that I was there and he could open his eyes and wake up. My brain had not quite wrapped itself around the fact that he had died. It was not my touching him that was the problem; it was that I allowed him to touch me. I do believe that when I tried to make him put his arms around me, some of the energy that was leaving his body transferred into mine. I say this because for the first few months after his death, I had an unusual sense of discomfort on the left side of my body, right around the hip area, right where his arm touched me as it fell away from my body. I first began to notice it in yoga class when I would experience quite a bit of discomfort on that side of my body. It felt as though Tasso was with me. The left side is the side I would always sleep on whenever he held out his arms for me to lay beside him. It was the only way I could explain it! It took me a minute to make the connection.

Our bodies are just masses of energy and this energy manifests itself in a form where we are able to see ourselves as physical beings. It made sense to me that his energy that was leaving his body transferred itself into my body, because I put his arm on me. This is why you must be careful. If the person that you let touch you is not close to you, you may not want this transference of energy to take place. I welcomed the discomfort as I considered it a part of him, but it is not something that I would generally recommend as it could have negative consequences depending on the person and the situation at their death. Over time, the discomfort has diminished and I believe it is because the energy has finally moved on from my body and transferred itself in the place where it was originally meant to be.

I think the reason I was able to experience these things is because our souls were in such tune with each other and with God. We were both very spiritual people and always had a strong belief and faith in God. We had been through enough in our lives together to know that we were able to overcome and achieve great things because God was always in control of our lives. It is something I think as humans, we tend to forget. We keep thinking that we are in control, but in reality, we are not! It is our responsibility to align ourselves with God so that we can fulfill what he has planned for us. I am grateful for the opportunities that have allowed me to be in touch with my spiritual self and with God. I am grateful for the pain and joys that each experience has brought to me!

Chapter Twenty-Six

I can see clearly that Tasso knew his death was coming. I don't know how far in advance he knew. I don't know why he didn't tell me – maybe he couldn't, maybe he wasn't supposed to.

Tasso got up every day, got dressed, and always had somewhere to go; something to do. I knew that he was slowing down in his normal everyday activity. I just thought he was finally listening to me when I would tell him that he didn't have to work so hard anymore. The kids were grown, he had finally gotten his 100% VA disability and his Social Security, and that income was enough for us to meet our basic needs and then some. Tasso always wanted and strived for more. I remember one day, he got up, got dressed, and then decided that all he wanted to do was take a nap. I remember telling him that he had been a wonderful husband, a great provider, and an amazing father, and if he never wanted to do anything for the rest of his life but get dressed and sleep all day, he had earned that right! I don't know why I used past tense. Maybe deep in my subconscious, I knew too!

In the last two weeks of his life, he went to visit his sister, then his brother, and a lifelong friend. They all told me that when he visited them, in general conversation, just out of the blue, he told them that he wasn't afraid to die. They thought it was unusual for him to talk that way, but they did not give it any further thought.

We were riding in the car one day, coming from North Fulton County where his sub-contractor had called him to pick up his share of a check from a completed job. We stopped for lunch, and on the way home, I told him (out of the blue this thought came to me) that I finally understood the concept of eternal life. I told him that people think of you living in this physical body forever, but that's not what it means. As long as you have children and grandchildren, I commented, you can never die! A part of you will live on in them forever and will continue in their children and their grandchildren. Anyone who knew Tasso knows that he loved a good philosophical, historical, religion-based conversation. I expected some type of conversation from him that day, but all he did was nod his head and say, "Um...", as if to say, now she's got it, she understands. I was surprised that he did not want to talk, but just dismissed it as him being in a rare, pensive mood.

I believe that the bird coming to the house and not responding to anyone except Tasso was an angel of death that was sent specifically to deliver a message from God to Tasso. God sent a bird because he knew I don't like birds. He knew if he sent a bird, I would not touch it! There is no other way I can explain it! Why else did Tasso "pet" the bird?! Why else was it such an odd looking bird?! It was only a short time after the appearance of the bird that Tasso asked to go to the hospital. I believe he wanted to go to the hospital so he would not die in the house. I guess he figured that might really be too hard for us to deal with!

Another thing, if Tasso had really wanted and needed some serious medical treatment, he would have asked to go downtown to Piedmont or Northside Hospital. He would have never consented to be taken to any of our local South Fulton County hospitals as they did not have the best reputation for giving out the best care. You would only go there if you were critical or in an accident and had to get to the closest place. I should have caught this one!

I am grateful that we had the sense of mind to have some life insurance. I only had taken out an insurance policy to have enough money to bury us. I only did this after Tasso came home from a relative's funeral and told me that a family member had commented that he hoped that no one would ask him for money to pay for the funeral. I decided I would never let us be put in that position and only took out a small policy for the both of us, just in case. Tasso always wanted me to take out one of those $500,000 life insurance policies on him (with me as the beneficiary, of course), but at our age, life insurance was expensive and I did not want to waste any of his money paying for some expensive life insurance policy that I figured we would never need. Our plan was to move to his land in Alabama, build us a house, and have the children come find us in bed asleep one day in each other's arms when we were in our 90's! That was our plan! I guess we forgot to consult with God about his plan!

When it came to talking about death and making funeral arrangements, the only thing Tasso would tell me was that he wanted an Islamic burial and he did not want to be buried in Loachapoka. I had

[163]

attended the funeral of a co-worker's mother years earlier and the service lasted about five hours and everybody under the sun got up and spoke about the deceased. I came home and told Tasso I wanted to make sure this would not happen to me! I wanted a short service, say a prayer, sing a song, put me in the ground, and go home and have a barbecue or party or something. I also joked about them not spending all of my money on some elaborate service. Take the money and go have a party! I even went so far as to write out the particulars of my service. I put all of that information into our safe. You see, for some reason, I was convinced that I would die before Tasso and I wanted everything to be in order.

One night, several months after we buried Tasso, I was going through some papers in the safe and discovered that the service I had written out for myself was almost the same exact service we had just held for Tasso! I was devastated! I blamed myself for Tasso's death! I had learned about the power of bringing things into existence by writing them down and I thought I had brought his death into existence by writing out a plan that I intended for myself! I became hysterical with grief and guilt! But then, wait... I had to remind myself, that while my words (spoken and written) may be powerful, they did not have the power to bring about life or death. It was a reality check! I was able to calm down and realize that I had no power to make anyone live or die. That is a power strictly reserved for God!

Part Six

And Now....

Chapter Twenty-Seven

After the funeral service, when all the friends and relatives had gone home, I was left to begin my new life without Tasso. My oldest son moved back home to help out and he settled into the garage apartment that Tasso had begun to use as his "man cave". In the midst of being emotionally distraught and heartbroken, I had to take care of business. I had to focus on finances and how I was going to be able to financially maintain my life and remain in our home. Since I had "retired" from my job at the end of 2006, Tasso was the sole support of our household. Now that he was gone, so was the money. I was unable to retain possession of the car, as I was unable to make the payments. I fell behind on the mortgage. I shared the funds from the life insurance policy with the children. I knew Tasso would have wanted me to do that and I felt it was the right thing to do. I paid cash for a car so I would have transportation without having to make a car payment and I used the rest to live on for as long as I could.

My brothers were very supportive and helped me out financially, but with their own families to support, their funds were limited. Besides, I would not have let them take me on as a dependent anyway. Tasso's family did not offer any type of support. After almost two years of negotiations, I was able to work out a deal with the bank where I could retain possession of our home. They were patient and waited until I could start receiving my VA death pension and Social Security.

The days and weeks that followed were emotionally difficult. I went through every emotion: sadness, anger, joy, depression, self-pity... You name it, and I felt it! I knew the children were watching me to see how I would deal with the situation. We were all in shock and in pain, but I felt like I had to set the example. I knew that having a complete emotional breakdown would serve no purpose. It would not bring Tasso back! Children listen to what you say, but they watch what you do even more, and I wanted to show them strength. Besides, Tasso hated to see me cry and I knew he would expect me to be strong and be a positive example for our children. Even more importantly than that, I felt that my actions and movements were being guided by God.

God's spirit and Tasso's spirit were all around me and guided my actions. That is the only way I can explain how I was able to function. However, there were times when I could do nothing but cry! My favorite place to do that was in the shower. I would turn the water on and just let it all out! I would moan and wail and sometimes I could not even recognize the sounds that came out of my mouth! It was as if every inch of my being, my heart, my soul, and my spirit was in pain! But, even reality creeped into those moments! I knew the water bill would be astronomical if I continued to take hour long showers, so eventually I knew I would have to cut those short! There would be place to hide or escape from this pain!

We tried for a while to keep Tasso's construction company up and running. Tasso had a couple of uncompleted jobs in the works at the time of his death and Ashuntu and Ishaaq stepped up to see those jobs to completion. We tried to do a couple of jobs on our own, but Tasso's work crews did not support us and we realized that we did not have the knowledge and skills that Tasso possessed to run a construction company. I guess we should have been paying more attention when Tasso was trying to teach us what to do! Needless to say, it was difficult for us to keep things going. Before Tasso died, he was in the process of retiring from the construction business. He had another project he was focusing his energy on with his land in Alabama. We decided to go ahead and dismantle Ossat Construction and focus more on the new company and the things Tasso wanted to accomplish through it. It is still a project that we intend to pursue in the future!

The first major life event occurred a week after we buried Tasso. My daughter, Ruby, and Jamaal's wife, were pregnant when Tasso died. Jamaal's baby was actually due to be delivered the day we buried Tasso, but her doctors postponed his delivery date for another week. On the 13th of November, one week after burying Tasso, we welcomed our newest member of the family into the world. Zion Michael Tasso was born! The following April, Ruby's son, Malik was born. Both boys have Tasso's name! (Malik was Tasso's Islamic name)!

I had joined a gym before Tasso died and had been active in Zumba and yoga, so I continued with my classes. They helped me keep in shape physically and mentally, and gave me a reason on most days to get out of bed. When I returned to the gym, and explained why I had been

[169]

absent for so many weeks, many of my "gym friends" showered me with love and support; sharing their stories of love and loss. One particular Zumba instructor had lost her husband several years before and she told me the first three years were the hardest. I looked at her and said, "the first three years!?" At that time, I could not even see my way past the first three months! It did not occur to me that I would have to face years without Tasso! It has been several years now since he has passed and I can clearly see what she meant.

The first three years, I think I was in shock. Just functioning, going through life, putting one foot in front of the other, trying to do what was required and expected. My physical mind knew that Tasso was gone, but for a long time, a part of me kept thinking and hoping it was all a dream. I wanted to wake up with him beside me so I could tell him what a nightmare I just had! Or, if I waited long enough, he would just come home like he always did. I even said that I would not even ask where he had been. I would just do like I normally did; fuss a little bit so he would know I missed him, tell him I was glad he was home, and ask him what he wanted me to cook for dinner! Or, I would be sitting in the backyard and I would hear the gate open; hear that booming voice, see that smile, and I would be excited to see what would be the next adventure we would engage in!

Life with Tasso was like an adventure. Every day was something new and different. You could not always know what to expect! But, in my mind I knew, none of that would happen. The problem was getting my head and my heart together on the same page. The head knew what was happening, the heart was much more reluctant. However, after the three year mark, it seemed as though the fog lifted, the head and heart got closer to being on the same page, and I finally started to admit to myself that I had a new life and it did not and would not ever again include Tasso! I would have to decide how I was going to live out the rest of my life without him.

One thing I had to do was finish my schoolwork. I only had five more weeks to go and I would be ready for graduation. When Tasso first died, I did not think I would be able to complete my coursework, but my children would not hear of me quitting. They told me that Dad did not go through everything he went through to get his VA benefits for me not to go ahead and finish my program. He would not want me to quit and I knew that they were right! I had to finish! I got myself together, and in December of 2013, my family and I went to Nashville where I received my Master's Degree in Counseling Studies. I was a graduate of Distinction (my GPA was 4.0)!

I was proud of myself that I had accomplished my goal. I was proud that my children got a chance to see me walk across that stage and receive my degree (the way we had watched all five of them do so many times)! At the same time, I was sad that Tasso was not there. I know he would have been grinning from ear to ear! It was because of his encouragement and support that I even had the courage to return to school after almost 40 years! He was my biggest supporter! He was always so positive and always instilled in me and our children that we could accomplish anything we wanted to if we just decided we wanted it and put some hard work behind it!

I had big plans for working in the counseling field, however, those plans changed! My life has taken a different direction and I have come to realize that God has a different plan for me other than the one I had anticipated. I had planned for Tasso and me to grow older and die in our sleep together. So much for my plan! It is best if you can get your life plan in accordance with what God has planned for you. That is the only way things work out, anyway!

Chapter Twenty-Eight

I have managed thus far to survive. I have managed to work out finances, so that I have enough to cover the basics. However, it has been difficult. Tasso always felt that I would be taken care of through spousal VA benefits, but because his death was not related to his disability (he died from a pulmonary embolism in his lung) and because it had not been ten years since he was rated 100% disabled, I was only granted a few hundred dollars of his pension. I inherited some of Tasso's entrepreneurial spirit and I started a little business for myself. I have always been a very neat and organized person and my children helped me realize that people will pay you to organize things for them. I have a few clients who call on me from time to time to help keep their belongings in order. We (I) have six grandchildren now and I enjoy babysitting them for their parents whenever they need me to and whenever I want to. All in all, I am able to keep myself busy and there are even moments when things feel "normal" again. Sometimes, in a few brief moments, I even think I have begun to feel joy!

In spite of all of my efforts to keep busy, I do get lonely. I think of Tasso and call his name every single day. I think he will always be alive in my heart. The worst times are at night. That was always the time when it was just the two of us. We would talk about out day's activities, or sometimes just be quiet. But that was always the time when it was just the two of us. That is when it dawns on me, again, that he is not physically here anymore. I think that most of my mourning was not so much about me losing him; it was more for me. I mourned the loss of Cynthia, the wife; Cynthia, the lover. Those people are gone. I cannot be his wife or lover anymore; that is a part of my life that I have to accept as over. I still sleep on his side of the bed, with my back turned to the side I used to sleep on. It is as if I am the one that died, not him. In a sense, a vital part of me did die.

I have now come to understand that Tasso was only on loan to us. I do believe that he was truly one of God's angels and he was put into my life to teach me lessons, help me find my true self, and to give me all the love I never felt when I was growing up. It may have been one of his missions. At any rate, he had fulfilled his work on this Earth and it was time for him to return home to God. Only God knows when our time is up and our journey on this earth is complete! Our job is to be ready when he calls us home!

As saddened as I am to be without him on this earth, I have to be happy that Tasso's earthly troubles and pains are over. I know that he was always in pain. From the time I met him, he told me about his back pain. He dealt with pain in his back every single day of his life that I knew him. I have only recently begun to understand chronic pain. I suffered minor knee and shoulder discomforts and sometimes they hurt for no reason at all! I am sure the pain I feel is minor in comparison to the pain Tasso must have endured in his back, but I do now have a clear understanding of what it must be like to be in pain all the time.

It has given me a whole new appreciation for the outstanding job that Tasso did as a man, working hard to provide for his family and taking time to be an active father to his children. I am sure there were so many times when we had him walking in the park and riding in the car, that his back must have really been hurting, but you would have never known it! He always had that big smile on his face and was one of happiest and most positive people I have ever known. I am so glad that I had a chance to tell him how much I loved him, respected him, and appreciated him for all that he did for us! (I told him stuff like that almost every day)! He definitely knew he was loved! I am glad that his pain and suffering are over!

I have often asked myself this question. What would I have done if God had offered me this choice? I can let Tasso stay on this earth with you, but he will suffer and be in constant pain OR I can bring him home with me and his pain and suffering will be over. What do you want me to do? I realized that I loved him so much that I would not want to see him hurt or be in pain and I would have had to answer, take him home. If you really, truly love someone, sometimes you have to put their well-being ahead of your own. I loved him that much that I would be willing to sacrifice my own happiness for his! I did that many times when he was alive!

Even still, I have to stop myself from mourning. If you believe in God, you cannot continue to mourn or grieve. Even though I wanted to die with Tasso (I always thought I would die before him), I had to realize that God left me here for a reason. I have to figure out what God wants me to do with the rest of my life and I have to get about the business of doing it. I want to be able to die peacefully like Tasso did. I want to be able to rest at home with God. Instead of moaning and being ungrateful, I have to be happy and thankful. I had the love of my life for 37 years. I deeply loved him and he deeply loved me. Some people will go through their whole lives and never experience the love and happiness that I shared with Tasso. Regardless of how painful it is, I have to focus more on what I gained, more than what I deemed I have lost.

I cannot lie to you, though. It is, by far, the hardest thing I have ever had to do in my life. I still feel as though my heart has been ripped out of my chest and is just a hole where my heart should be. When I first went back to yoga, there is a move where you bring your hands to your heart center. I literally could not do it! I could not feel my heart, there was no center! The only thing I could think of to do that would help ease the pain was to pray. I prayed all the time! (I still do!) I am just one big ball of prayer! I am so glad that God does not give us a number limit on the number of times we can pray because I'm pretty sure I would have used all of mine up a long time ago! I just keep on praying, keep on living, and I keep trying to get it right. I use every day that I wake up as another chance to show God that I can honor and glorify him in my thoughts, words, and, deeds, and that he did not make a mistake when he created me. I will spend the rest of my days trying to prove myself worthy of his love. I hope to be able to find my place with Him in his heavenly palace when my life here is done.

I have read that when this life is over, and if you have lived good enough to make it back to God's heavenly home, you will be reunited with those who you have had a strong connection with through love with on this earth. I look forward to seeing my beloved Tasso again!

A few family photos from the early days

Family photos with the "babies" all grown up!

[179]

Part Seven

Poems

Chapter Twenty-Nine

The first poem I wrote, "Every Day", came to me one day as I was thinking that every day since Tasso died, I missed him, I cried, I called his name…it evolved into a poem. It was written in 2014. The others came to me as a result of me trying to understand, express, and make some sense of his death and the profound sense of loss I was experiencing. They were all written in 2015, with the exception of "Just When" which was written in 2016, and "Now" which was written in 2017. One day, when I felt that I had crossed some milestone in my grieving process, I looked at all of the poems that I had written and realized that they actually have chronicled my journey through my grieving process….thus far! I want to share them with you!

Every Day

Every day I miss you
Every day I cry
Every day I'm lonely
Every day I ask why
Every day I'm sad
Every day I'm blue
Every day I'm feeling lost
Because I don't have you

Every day I want you
Every day I need you
Every day I wonder
How I'll live without you

And even though I'm hurting

And even though I'm blue

Every day I'm glad
I shared my life with you!

My Thoughts of You

No matter where I go
No matter what I do
There is no way to escape
My thoughts of you

Whether dark or bright
Whether day or night
There is no way to escape
My thoughts of you

I love you so
You have to know
There is no way to escape
My thoughts of you
Whether happy or sad
Whether good or bad
There is no way to escape
My thoughts of you!

<u>Without You</u>

I eat, I sleep
I walk, I talk
I laugh, I cry
The days go by

But it's not the same
No one to blame
It's all a part of this game we play
called Life!

The joys, the pains

The sunshine, the rain

The tears, the fears

Make up the years
I now must live

Without You!

It's hard to know
How it will go?
Which path to take?
What difference will it make?

Now that I have to do it all

Without You!

I Miss...

I miss
Your eyes that used to see me
Your hands that used to touch me
Your heart that beat with mine
Your spirit that kept me alive

I miss
Your arms that used to hold me
Your lips that used to kiss me
Your ears that always heard me
Your tears that mixed with mine

I miss
Your smile that used to warm me
Your words that used to inspire me
Your voice that used to greet me
Your calm that used to comfort me

I miss
Everything about you
My heart forever belongs to you
You are the best thing I ever knew
I will never, ever forget you!

It Hurts

My heart..........can't beat.......... it hurts

My head..........can't think........... it hurts

My soul...........can't feel............it hurts

My spirit..........can't breathe.......it hurts

My body..........can't move.........it hurts

My mind..........can't be free....... it hurts

In all I say

In all I do

I feel the loss of you

And
It hurts!
But if this hurt I feel
Is the price I must pay
For loving you
Then
It is hurt
I will gladly bear
The rest of my days!

<u>Just When</u>

Just when I thought I couldn't miss you any more....
I do!
Just when I thought I couldn't love you any more....
I do!
Just when I thought I couldn't want you any more....
I do!
Just when I thought I couldn't cry any more....
I do!
Just when I thought I wouldn't hurt any more....
I do!
Just when I thought I wouldn't need you any more....
I do!

You are me......
I am you......
Death has not done us part....
...not in my heart
I still do!

<u>Now</u>

I miss you so much
It's hard to explain
The sadness I feel
Or the depth of my pain

My head knows you're gone
My brain understands
My heart's not the same
Keeps waiting for you
To walk through the door
And take away all the pain!

Sometimes I still cry
Try not to ask why
Just doesn't seem fair
No one seems to care
What I say or what I do
If or how I get through!

I close my eyes and remember
the touch of your hands
the warmth of your smile
the sound of your voice
the sparkle in your eyes

I love you so
Know I have to let go
And just when I think I'm through
My heart tells me, 'it's not true!"
So I'll just keep on trying
To keep from crying
Focus on living, not dying
Until we meet again!

[197]

One of the few photos we have taken together as a family since Tasso's death

Me and the grandbabies!

2017 Thomas Family Tree

How Our Love Has Grown

Tasso
(deceased)

Cynthia

Ashuntu

Ruby

Jamaal

Jamilah

Ishaaq

Tenisio

Shannan

Leroy

Kwame

Malik

Zaiden

Zuri

Zion

Scarlett